"At least since Monta.
ence when it comes
Parkison is in fine for   ...gtal church and
western culture at large ... ue balance. His muscular and direct
approach is just what we need in this age when mollifying the
truth and pacifying the church are the prevailing strategies for
'winning the world.' I enjoyed this collection immensely."

C.R. Wiley
Author of *The Household and the War for the Cosmos:*
Recovering a Christian Vision for the Family

"I will never forget the rush that came from first reading great
Christian minds like C.S. Lewis, Francis Schaeffer, and G.K. Chesterton. It didn't matter whether they were writing about the hypo-
static union, a splattered Jackson Pollock canvas, or cheese... They
opened up expansive vistas for me to behold the shine of Christ's
Lordship over all of life. Samuel Parkison is carrying the torch of
these luminaries. His book *Thinking Christianly* does exactly what
its subtitle promises, *Bringing Sundry Thoughts Captive to Christ*.
Whether he is pondering preferred pronouns, warning of the
woes of transhumanism, unearthing landmines on social media
battlefields, contemplating the contagious wonder of children, or
ruminating about racism, Parkison's writing will pull you into a
much larger world. It will give you a fresh sense of the joy, cour-
age, humility, and wonder that come from taking every thought
captive to the Lord Jesus."

Thaddeus J. Williams
Professor of Systematic Theology at Talbot School of Theology;
author of *Confronting Injustice Without Compromising Truth: 12 Questions*
Christians Should Ask About Social Justice

"Whether he is exposing the unbiblical foundations of critical race theory, gay marriage, and transgenderism, or warning against the dangers of envy, cancel culture, and transhumanism, Samuel Parkison writes with the penetrating wit of Chesterton, the ecumenical embrace of C. S. Lewis, and the heart of a pastor who has grieved over the confusion, despair, and brokenness of his young parishioners."

Louis Markos
Professor in English and Scholar in Residence Houston Baptist University; author of *Atheism on Trial: Refuting the Modern Arguments Against God*

"Samuel G. Parkison writes with naked candour as he applies biblical wisdom and 'not-so-common' sense to a range of perplexing and controversial issues facing 21st-century Christians. Parkison's candour is coupled with a colloquial style and a genuine pastoral concern for his readers, as he offers practical approaches to the complex and nuanced landscape of postmodernism, woke ideology, and relativism. This book is a veritable grab-bag of disarming, down-to-earth wisdom, as well as timely insights in the timeless and ever illuminating vein of the works of Harry Blamires, Francis Schaeffer, C.S. Lewis, and G.K. Chesterton, *et al.* Not only does Parkison reflect these great luminaries in his essays, he also harkens his audience to read 'upstream'—that is, to read the writers and thinkers he makes mention of, intellectual giants such as C.S. Lewis, Alexander Solzhenitsyn, Herman Bavinck, Thomas Aqinas, Cornelius Van Til, and Roger Scruton. In doing so, he not only helps us to think *rightly* about our contemporary context, he also teaches us how to think rightly as a *Christian* in every situation—past, present, and future."

Jeremy W. Johnston
Adjunct professor of rhetoric at Heritage College and Seminary; author of *All Things New: Essays on Christianity, culture and the arts*

"As these essays reveal, Samuel Parkison is a refreshing thinker. For these are thoughtful essays that stem from a solidly biblical worldview and demand thought and not the parroting of a party-line. And they are fresh takes on important issues that, read rightly, lead to refreshment of soul and spirit. Ideal for those who want a quick read and a long train of thought."

Michael A.G. Haykin
Chair and Professor of Church History,
The Southern Baptist Theological Seminary

Thinking Christianly

To Glen,

For thinking Christianly,
for helping me to think Christianly,
and for the conversations that occasioned many of these essays.

Thank you.

THINKING
CHRISTIANLY

BRINGING SUNDRY THOUGHTS
CAPTIVE TO CHRIST

SAMUEL G. PARKISON

Thinking Christianly
Copyright © Samuel G. Parkison 2022

All rights reserved. This book or any portion thereof may not be reproduced or used in any manner whatsoever without the express written permission of the publisher except for the use of brief quotations in a book review.

Published by: Joshua Press, Peterborough, Ontario
www.JoshuaPress.com

Front cover design by Samuel G. Parkison

Paperback ISBN: 978-1-77484-059-7
Ebook ISBN: 978-1-77484-060-3

Contents

A Word to the Reader

This book should be read in the spirit of 2 Corinthians 10:4–5: "For the weapons of our warfare are not of flesh but have divine power to destroy strongholds. We destroy arguments and every lofty opinion raised against the knowledge of God, and take every thought captive to obey Christ." It does not pretend to be exhaustive in its contents, it is rather an example of thinking Christianly about a sampling of issues. If the topics appear to be haphazardly picked, it is because they were: most of these essays had previous iterations that were featured on small blogs (chiefly, my own and my church's) over the course of several years. While I have worked to refashion them appropriately as a collection of essays in book form, they were not originally written with an eye toward publication. What you see here is a Christian's attempt to think Christianly, and a pastor's attempt to help his congregation think Christianly. The issues considered here in this book are the issues that, at some point or another, demanded my own attention as a Christian, a dad, a husband, a pastor, a neighbor. Therefore, you should read each piece as a stand-alone essay. If there is one unifying theme to the book as a whole, it is the ever relevance of Christ's lordship. Beyond that, searching for robust cohesion is destined to end in frustration, so I would not recommend that.

Two other words of clarification might be helpful. First, as it relates to the tone of this book, readers may be tempted to conclude from many of the essays that the author is a cynic. I should like to think this conclusion would be misunderstood, even if understandable. This book is not a polemic *per se*, but it certainly does have much polemical content therein. This is not because I get out of bed in the morning, and with a spring in my step, dive into another day of torching people with whom I disagree. I hope I am not wrong to say the activity of reveling in gospel truth is more central to my life than criticizing bad Christian-thinking. But this book attempts to bring "sundry thoughts captive to Christ," which means the thoughts I'm concerned with here are typically *not* already captive to Christ. These are wily, runaway thoughts running amuck, needing to be wrangled in. The critical tone is, I believe, proportionate to the content.

Second, I should like to tip my hat to the chief influences on this book. Head and shoulders above the rest are G.K. Chesterton and C.S. Lewis. I am more indebted than I can articulate to those ancient-modernists, those Medievalists, those gluttons for life and tellers of truth. Probably every meaningful insight in this book is accidentally plagiarized from them, and probably every error in my thinking they have criticized in some way.

While I'm on the theme of offering blanket plagiarism-protection hedges, let me also acknowledge the substantial (conscious and sub-conscious) influence of Douglas and N.D. Wilson, whom I regard as children of Lewis and grandchildren of Chesterton (I cannot resist pointing out that I am calling Wilson the elder and Wilson the younger *Calvinist* progeny of Lewis and Chesterton, which probably would have frustrated Chesterton enough to write a hilarious essay, and would have tickled Lewis enough to write a warm-hearted letter). Lastly, I wish to recognize the influence of the Puritans; those oft slandered soul-doctors of the Church. For all of these lovers of truth and lovers of God, I am profoundly grateful.

Samuel G. Parkison
Kansas City, Missouri.
November, 2020.

Chapter 1
No Fear, No Wisdom

People often believe the book of Proverbs is a spiritually neutral collection of helpful insights. As if what was collected therein were simple truisms that lay out on the ground for whoever happens to stumble across them. If Solomon happens to find wisdom in one place, it is because he just so happens to have been looking *there*, while Confucius was looking *here*, and Oprah was looking *elsewhere*. But assuming such is a grave misunderstanding. This is not how the book of Proverbs works. One does not, we are told explicitly, tap into this book's insight without "fear of the LORD."

But who is this LORD whom philosophers (i.e., all who would "love wisdom") are invited to fear? Although we are familiar with the word "Lord," our English translations do not do us a service by using it in this context, for Proverbs tells us plainly enough *who* it is we must come to fear if we desire wisdom, and it is not anyone who happens to wear the general title of "Lord." Those capital letters bespeak a name. "L-O-R-D" is the stand-in for God's covenant name: *Yahweh*. So the path to true wisdom is not reverence for *a god* in general; it is reverence for Israel's covenant-making God. The fear of "Yahweh" is the beginning of wisdom.

But if this is true, its implied converse is quite striking. If fearing God is the beginning of wisdom, then the refusal to fear God is the beginning of all folly. The essence of folly, then, is something along the lines of "trying to live in God's world without conforming to God's will." Now, the reality is that God is incredibly gracious, and he keeps "fools" from consistently living according to their folly. God-fearers and God-despisers live in the same world, created and sustained with the same symmetry and design imbedded therein by the same God. The fool who says in his heart that there is no God still lives in God's cosmos, and try as he may, there is nothing he can do about its being God's. He is like the rebellious adolescent who hates his parents and declares, "I don't need you!"—while living in his parents' house, which is insured by his parents' employer, where he sleeps on the bed his parents bought, eating food in the refrigerator his parents' stock, bashing his parents online with a phone they provided using the internet services for which they pay. As unflattering as it sounds, this is the "fool" who says in his heart, "there is no God"—he is living in God's world, receiving all his benefits, while denying that he is in fact the benefactor.

Incidentally this is why, on the surface level, some of the insights we receive from Proverbs may be universally accessible to Christian and non-Christian alike. The Christian and the non-Christian both live in the world the Triune God created and sustains. While their ultimate commitments differ, their eyeballs see the same stuff. But this does not mean that there is such a thing as *neutral* wisdom, because there is, in fact, no such thing as *neutral anything*. All truth is God's truth. God-despisers do grasp truth on account of what the Protestant Reformers referred to as "common notions" (i.e., genuine truths about God and morality that believers and non-believers alike may deduce from the world around them), but it's all still *God's* truth they grasp.[1] Whether God-despisers acknowledge this fact or not is beside the point. "All things were created through him and *for him*," says Paul to the Colossians. No, the non-Christian who experiences the surface-level insights of Proverbs understands not its fullest wisdom. There is all the difference in the world between seeing a street-sign and *reading* a street-sign. "Learning how to read," so to speak,

---

[1] This idea of "common notions" is what the Canons of Dort refer to as "the light of nature," which remains "in all people after the fall, by virtue of which they retain some notions about God, natural things, and the difference between what is moral and immoral, and demonstrate a certain eagerness for virtue and for good outward behavior." Canons of Dort, Third and Fourth Main Points of Doctrine, Article IV, in *The Three Forms of Unity* (Moscow, ID: Canon Press, 2021), 69.

comes from covenantal allegiance and reverence. Or, to bring back our earlier analogy, a rebellious teenager may have some insight on how to navigate a smart phone his parents bought him, but that does not make him wise. He does not *understand* that smart phone like the grateful teenager in right relationship with his parents—the teenager who understands his gift *in relation* to its giver. The ungrateful one understands that it is a combination of metal and glass and wires and is a work of technological genius, but he does not know that it is a *gift*, and he therefore does not know it in wisdom.

True wisdom—biblical wisdom—is not limited to the intellect. It certainly includes the intellect, but what we are talking about is the difference between knowing what a star *is* and what a star is *made of*. We need to learn the lesson Lewis wrote for his character Eustace, speaking with the Narnian Star, Ramandu:

> "In our world," said Eustace, "a star is a huge ball of flaming gas."
>
> "Even in your world, my son, that is not what a star is but only what it is made of."[2]

Lady Wisdom does not invite you to come into her house and lounge as you pontificate and speculate about the deep mysteries of the universe, unattached. She certainly does invite you to think about those things deeply, but in the context of eating and drinking and laughing and sleeping and cleaning up the dishes and folding the laundry. Her lessons are not disembodied concepts one can entertain intellectually but never practice. Her lessons connect the food that elicits joy to the true Source of joy, and insists that you have not understood the former until basking in the

---

[2] C.S. Lewis, *The Voyage of the Dawn Treader* (New York: NY, Harper Collins, 2002), 115.

glow of the latter. Biblical wisdom is concerned with the whole person, wholly living before the face of God. Right thinking and right living are the two hands of a wise person, who uses those hands in reverent service to God.

And this God is known truly and finally to the Christian alone, for this God is the Triune God who comes to us in the Person of Jesus—Emmanuel— "God with us." There is therefore a uniquely wise—a uniquely Christian—way of doing *everything*. When we talk with our neighbors, instruct our children, eat our meals, do the dishes, engage on social media, think about politics, date, spend our money, sexually engage our spouse, receive insults, save for retirement—we should be thinking, "What is the uniquely wise—uniquely Christian—way of doing this?" We can be certain the proper answer, whatever it is, is never that there is no uniquely Christian way.

Let us consider one example. If we ask, "What is the uniquely Christian way of engaging on social media?" Lady wisdom answers, "The way of a fool is right in his own eyes, but a wise man listens to advice" (Prov. 12:16), and "The vexation of a fool is known at once, but the prudent ignores an insult" (12:17), and "Whoever is slow to anger has great understanding, but he who has a hasty temper exalts folly" (14:29), and "A soft answer turns away wrath, but a harsh word stirs up anger" (15:1), and "Pride goes before destruction, and a haughty spirit before a fall" (16:18), and "Whoever covers an offense seeks love, but he who repeats a matter separates close friends" (17:9), and "A fool gives full vent to his spirit, but a wise man quietly holds it back" (29:11).

Lady Folly, on the other hand, sings a very different tune. The most brazen form of Lady Folly's message can be found in Proverbs 7, or 9:13–18:

> The woman Folly is loud;
>   she is seductive and knows nothing.

She sits at the door of her house;
    she takes a seat on the highest places of the town,
calling to those who pass by,
    who are going straight on their way,
"Whoever is simple, let him turn in here!"
    And to him who lacks sense she says,
"Stolen water is sweet,
    and bread eaten in secret is pleasant."
But he does not know that the dead are there,
    that her guests are in the depths of Sheol.

"You will get away with it," she says, "you will enjoy it. Live life with no regrets—today, gratify your desires." But this is not her only speech. Notice that the heart of her strategy is to expose and exploit one's sinful desires—she *affirms* us in our folly. Which means much deeper than the explicit temptation to disobey is the idolatry of *self*. Sometimes she focuses on the end—i.e., "*break this law of God's because you deserve it*." And sometimes she focuses on the means without explicitly mentioning the end—i.e., "you deserve everything." But starting there cannot but lead to the same deathly end.

It is therefore important that we learn to recognize the tone of Lady Folly's voice in whatever context we happen to find ourselves. Her invitations persist as long as we live in this world, east of Eden. And she borrows the lips of many a witless sap. Her words were found on the lips of Satan with the question, "Did God actually say, 'You shall not eat of any tree in the garden'?" and in his statement, "You will not surely die. For God knows that when you eat of it your eyes will be opened, and *you will be like God*, knowing good and evil" (Gen. 3:1, 4–5). You can hear her voice today still, as well. She asks questions like:

Does not God simply want you to be happy?
Did not God make you this way?
Is this not your body?
Is this not freedom?

Is this not your choice?
Ought you not cut out toxic people?
Ought you not prioritize self-care? If you don't who will?
Ought you not go, girl?
Are you not your own master?

This is serious business, and Lady Folly has no shortage of party guests, even among those who follow Christ. One ought not presume that one is beyond succumbing to her invitations just because one may reject outright these *explicit* "proverbs of Folly." She invites implicitly and under cover too.

She does so in the Rom Com that depicts when the fornicating couple overcomes all odds to find true love—when prudence is thrown to the wind, marriages are destroyed, God's law is despised, bridges are burned, but you are expected to celebrate because the two guilty parties finally found true happiness. She offers her invitation to our children in every animated movie that sells the diabolical lie that the ultimate vice is "self-denial," while the ultimate virtue is to "follow one's heart." She invites in the deep recesses of your mind when you harbor resentment for your spouse for failing to recognize your all-importance. She is a sneaky, wily, devious little thing, and you must learn to recognize her invitations for what they are.

And if we want to know where to look, alternatively, to find the homely house of Lady Wisdom instead of the dark den of Lady Folly, we ought to look no further than the Logos himself—Jesus Christ. The road forks at Jesus. To reject Jesus is to reject wisdom. It is an oxymoron to be wise, according to biblical standards, whilst persisting in refusal to submit to Jesus. The fear of the LORD is the beginning of wisdom, and we fear God through Jesus. Lady Wisdom invites us to come her way, fearing God, and Jesus tells us, "I am the way, the truth, and the life, no one comes to the Father except by me" (Jn. 14:6). It is not for nothing that until very recently, when chronological snobbery and modernistic reductionism took deep root in biblical scholarship, virtually all pre-modern biblical interpreters read Lady Wisdom's speech in Proverbs 8 as the personified voice of Jesus Christ himself. Indeed, one has to try mightily to read Proverbs 8 and John 1:1-18 and *not* recognize Jesus—the pre-existent Word, the Wisdom of God—as the common subject of both passages. Lady Wisdom is a poetic personification of God's wisdom—but *all the treasures of wisdom and knowledge are hidden in Christ.* You cannot get God's wisdom without coming to Jesus.

Chapter 2
On (Not) Attending Same-Sex "Weddings"

Although King Solomon was not wrong when he warned us that there is nothing new under the sun, the sense of novelty still comes along and jolts us awake from time to time. The phenomenon of homosexual erotic activity, for example, is not new. What *is* new is the social impulse to consecrate it as sacred "marriage." What we have here, is the combination of several old things to make one sort of new thing. Sexual anarchy is old, the religious impulse to sanctify sexual expression is old, but the notion of "gay marriage" is certainly not old. Old in essence, new in form.

In contemplating how Christians should respond to such a phenomenon, a base-level conviction should be to decline to attend these ceremonies when invited. I understand that what I consider here as "base-level" is not a widely shared conviction, so I will here take nothing for granted. I shall argue my case for you.

The most fundamental reason Christians should decline invitations to "same-sex weddings" is that such "weddings" are no weddings at all. As Christians, the Bible is our final authority for faith and practice, especially with regard to topics that it itself explicitly addresses; and the Bible is not silent on marriage. It is the covenant union between one man and one woman, joined together by God himself (Gen. 2:18–25, Matt. 19:3–9, Eph. 5:22–33). The legal union between two people of the same sex may be something, but it will never be marriage. Marriage is something that has been established by God, and it is woven into the very fabric of reality.

But what about Romans 13? Are we not supposed to be subject to our governing authorities? The answer should be, "of course," but only within the sphere over which said authorities have rightful sovereignty. If I come to discover that congress has passed a bill to annul the law of gravity, I would not celebrate by walking off a building. Congress has no authority over the law of gravity. The same is true with regard to marriage; it is an untouchable reality. No sooner could congress (or in the case of the United States, the Supreme Court *playing* congress) establish a law that triangles have four sides.

But, of course, to say that marriage is woven into the fabric of the natural order is to insist on the very unpopular notion that there is such a thing as a "natural order." As unfashionable as it is to bring up the latter half of Romans chapter one in this discussion, it really does inform us, not just about same-sex "weddings," but about homosexuality in general. What Romans 1 tells us is that when you cut yourself off from God—the source of all wisdom—you cannot but become *foolish*. When you cut yourself off from the Light of holiness, your heart cannot but become darkened.

It also tells us about the centrality of worship in this discussion. The presence of indwelling sin is not manifested in the refusal to worship. It is manifested in the refusal to worship *God*. "Whatever I worship," says fallen humanity, "I will not worship God." And thus, we exchange the glory of God for images resembling mortal man and birds and animals and creeping things. We worship and serve the creature rather than the Creator. We worship anything but God. We should therefore not be surprised when we see our culture's current drift into paganism. We worship nature, we worship power and political capital, we worship money, we worship sex, we worship our pets, we worship ourselves, all because we will not worship God, and the worshiping impulse we are irreducibly strapped with abhors a vacuum.

Now, this is all well and good conceptually, but what does it have to do with attending same-sex "weddings" in the twenty-first century? Everything, in fact. Paul is building a case that God is justified in revealing wrath from heaven against all ungodliness, and he points to widespread idolatry as the justification for—and *manifestation of*—divine wrath. And when he intends to cite a clear, obvious, brazen example to prove his point, the practice of homosexuality is the example to which he appeals. This is because it is a stark display of man's rejection of God's authority. They who affirm the virtue of homosexuality eschew the "natural relations" embedded in the cosmos by God, because God put them there.

I suppose I am stating the obvious by saying that this is profoundly countercultural. Our increasingly pagan society insists that sexual desire is the defining characteristic of a person, and that to disparage one's sexual desires or sexual expression is to disparage their very humanity. It insists also that such desires exist on a spectrum, and there is no such thing as "natural relations." "You be you," "you speak your truth," is the sentiment of our culture. But Paul's words, ploughing furiously in the opposite direction, show that God has created the world to function in a particular way. There is a natural order of things. And wisdom labors to seek it out, and harmonize with it. Wisdom says, "What is my part? What is my harmony? When do I come in? When do I quiet down? Let me contribute to the symphony of creation." To do so is to honor God as the Creator. Lest we get too far away from our topic, let me say it plainly: sexual desire has a natural order. It exists to be expressed within the context of marriage between a man and woman. That is what sexuality is *for*.

But when humanity cuts itself off from God, when it suppresses the truth in unrighteousness and exchanges the truth about God for the lie, disorder follows. It cannot *not* follow. The more consistent fallen man is in his rejection of God's authority, the more he will rage against his natural order, since it reflects him whom he hates. This is why an increasingly godless society is an increasingly anti-natural-order society (regardless of how much it boasts of being "scientific"). If God is God, and I am not, then my sexuality exists for what he made it for. If God is God, and I am not, then my gender is what God says it is. If God is God, and I am not, marriage is what he calls it, and not what I dream up. If God is God, and I am not, there is a givenness to creation that cannot be manipulated by my sheer will, because *I do not have the authority or the ability to make the boundaries budge.* They are fixed.

The person who hates God cannot abide these things. The society that hates God will reject God's order at every possible turn. "Humanity is what *I* say it is. The unborn baby has the value *I* attribute to it. *My* sexual desires are intrinsically virtuous because they are *mine.* My gender is what *I* say it is—it is a social construct, nothing more. Marriage is what *I* say it is—and *I* say it is an egalitarian partnership; husbandly headship does not jive with me. Heterosexual, monogamous marriage does not jive with me." This is what godlessness says to God's authoritative ordering. It turns its nose at nature.

But the world is what God made it to be, and no matter how hard we try in our sinfulness, we cannot wish away the boundaries of the natural world. To borrow from an earlier illustration, if I say I reject the natural order of gravity and jump off a building, I may have the sensation of freedom for a moment, but the reality of the pavement will not respect "my truth." It obeys God and God alone, and he commands for it to be solid, and for gravity to continue to pull me down.

This, of course, does not mean that everyone who experiences same-sex attraction experiences them because they are consciously hating God. Regenerate saints of Christ can and do experience such attraction. But such attractions are, manifestly, "contrary to nature," and are present because of the fall. This means that the recent trend of Christians insisting on celibacy whilst maintaining a "gay identity" makes as little sense as the man who celebrates his Pedophilia as an identity whilst insisting that he keeps his hands to himself at the playground. You cannot claim the identity of Christ and also the identity of the sin and sinfulness that put him on the cross. To be alive in Christ is to be dead to sin. This does not mean that the Christian never deals with "the old man" trying to get up out of the grave, but it does certainly mean that the Christian has no business trying to reconcile that sinful zombie with his new resurrection life in Christ.

So Christians should not attend same-sex weddings because to do so is to lie—to confirm one's neighbors in the delusion that they do in fact have the independence from God they have declared. But on another level, attending such a "wedding" is to celebrate sin. We are there to solemnize and affirm the union; that is what we do when we attend weddings; it is supposed to be a joyous occasion. Which is why traditional weddings have that bit that says, "If anyone has any objections to this union, speak now or forever hold your peace;" the silence that follows is the affirmation of the union. However, if the Bible is correct about sin, the "wedding" of a same-sex couple is not a joyous occasion. It is a tragedy and mockery. What is the Christian attendee supposed to do when the official says, "I now pronounce you husband and husband?" Is he to clap? Is he to weep?

"Yes, yes, but what about evangelism?" says the well-meaning would-be attendee, "What if I go there to show the love of Jesus; to show some grace?" At first blush, this line of argument may ring with self-evident truth. After all, did not Jesus hang out with sinners? Did not Paul say that it is not the sexually immoral of this world that Christians are to distance ourselves from?

Let us not be hasty in the assumption that these examples give us license to attend a celebration of sin. There is all the difference in the world between associating with sinners and affirming their sins. Attending a birthday party is not the same thing as attending a wedding. We should remember that the Paul who instructs us to associate with the sexually immoral of this world—who became "all things to all people, that by all means [he] might save some"— is the same Paul who strictly forbade Roman Christians to join in the pagan drinking parties (which would turn into orgies) that were prevalent in their particular culture (Rom. 13:13–14). Becoming all things to all people does not, evidently, involve the celebration of all peoples' sin.

Further, a Christian's presence at a same-sex "wedding" is actually not helping his witness; it does the opposite, in fact. Rather than bringing the gospel to a same-sex "wedding," the Christian attendee is actually undermining it by his presence. The gospel is only sweet to those who consider the taste of sin to be bitter. Jesus says, "Those who are well have no need of a physician, but those who are sick. I have not come to call the righteous but sinners to repentance" (Lk. 5:31–32). A sinner will never repent if he sees no sin to repent of. A sick man will never seek a physician if he thinks himself healthy. Paul says, "Therefore, we are ambassadors for Christ, God making his appeal through us. We implore you on behalf of Christ, be reconciled to God" (2 Cor. 5:20). When we beg people to be reconciled to God, we are presupposing that reconciliation is necessary. It is in the contrast of sin's depravity that the grace of God shines more brilliantly. The darker the night, the brighter the dawn. We cannot come to appreciate the grace of God until we reckon with the sinfulness of sin. And our appreciation for the grace of God in the gospel will rise and fall with our appreciation of his holiness and thereby, the severity of our sin. The holier he is in our minds, the graver our sin will be, and the graver our sin, the more exquisite the gospel.

So when we refuse to identify sin—with our words or with our actions—we are not being "gospel centered." Rather, we are robbing the gospel of its potency. The crucifixion was not God's way of ignoring sin.

On (Not) Attending Same-Sex "Weddings"

The fragrance we give off as Christians will always smell sweet to some, and horrible to others (2 Cor. 4:14–17). The Holy Spirit alone can convict sinners of sin, and turn the repulsive, foolish message we preach into good news for them. But our job is simple; we are heralds. We proclaim that sinners need salvation from their sin, and that God has provided it in the person and work of his Son. We give off the aroma of Christ, and we let the chips fall where they may. We will never experience the delight of being the sweet aroma of life to those who are being saved until we are willing to be the stench of death to those who are perishing.

Chapter 3
The Danger of Cool-Shaming[1]

It appears as though the fall of the evangelical Church in America may not happen with a bang. To go out with a bang implies a conflict of some sort, but conflict requires unction, and I confess I do not see much of that these days. I see more of a pacified self-sorting by many who calculate their positions on social and moral and political issues based on what they anticipate their unbelieving neighbors will approve of. For such, the only moments of fight come when they muster up the strength to rebuke Christians who are not self-sorting with them.

What lies behind such an impulse to self-sort? To be over anxious not so much about being truthful or faithful, but rather about being relevant? We may be tempted to conclude that the answer comes from a pragmatic desire for institutional growth, but I do not think that is it. For one thing, the sort of voluntary bondage to worldliness I have in mind here has not proven to be a good strategy for numerical growth in churches. It is true that big evangelical churches that begin the drift into worldliness often experience rapid growth, but more often than not, that growth comes from other evangelicals who have been flirting with worldliness for some time and desire some spiritual vindication for their love interest.

Evidently, there is a huge demand for waystations that allow for Christians to ease their way into worldliness (instead of jumping in with both feet). Booming evangelical churches that pick up the world's newspeak surrounding justice or sexual ethics or tolerance broadcast to such individuals: *All ye who enter here shall find a safe place to make thy transition into worldliness slowly.*

---

[1] I am indebted to Doug Wilson for this phrase.

But we have seen this trend happen often enough to know that the attendance spike is temporary. At some point, the church becomes indistinguishable from the political party or the activist group or the university classroom, and attendees wise up to the pointlessness of attending a non-church and quietly walk away. And who can blame them? So, no, the reason for the self-sorting is probably not at base a desire to grow in numbers. It is worse than that. It is a craven lust for approval. It is a self-inflicted "cool-shame" occasioned by an insatiable fear of man. But here, I must take some time to give some examples of the kind of thing I have in mind, lest I be accused of leaning against windmills. Let me consider two examples in turn.

Sexual Ethics
Many evangelicals are getting squishy on issues Scripture portray as solid and firm. I once watched an evangelical mega-church pastor squirm for five solid minutes in a TV interview, wherein he resolutely refused to answer the question of homosexuality and sin. His defense was something along the lines of, "I cannot tell a person what they must or must not do. That's their journey." Meanwhile, the TV host pressed him, suggesting that perhaps, given his position as a *pastor*, he had a moral imperative to tell people what *the Bible* had to say. Apparently not, according to this pastor.[2] Anecdotal though this example may be, I am quite sure the example does not surprise anyone, and the absence of shock is the point exactly.

While evangelicals may not be out front on the cutting edge of praising the sexual revolution, the position they do occupy is no less egregious and not a little embarrassing. They are dragging on behind, looking furtively at the pagans who *are* on the cutting edge, just praying for them to turn around and notice their efforts

---

[2] "Carl Lentz with Katie Couric 12:14," *YouTube* (Published on June 4, 2014. https://www.youtube.com/watch?v=_3wLm6pPvRY. Accessed on November 3, 2020)

to distance themselves from those *fundamentalists*. If that magical
moment happens, such evangelicals do not want the risk of being
associated with the sort of players that might scare the pagan off,
taking his precious approval with him. Which is why the loudest
opposition to bold, prophetic Christian witness against sexual sin
most often comes not from our unbelieving neighbors, but from
concerned evangelicals who are speaking *on behalf of* unbelieving
neighbors. Fancying themselves the brave boy on the schoolyard
who defends the young damsel (i.e., the hypothetical unbeliever)
from the bully (i.e., "fundamentalists"), their actual condition is
quite pitiful. In reality, the pagan sees no difference between the
fundamentalist and the "culturally sensitive" one. The latter's efforts to distance himself from the former are futile, so long as he
cannot give a firm and resolute affirmative to the question: "Can
girls become boys?" Anything shy of a hearty, "Yes!" is going to
place him alongside the fundamentalist in the estimation of the
pagan, whether he likes it or not (incidentally, the fundamentalist
is no more happy about this association than the "culturally sensitive" evangelical, but he at least knows there's nothing to be done
about it). But the moment a "Yes!" is rendered, the relevant evangelical just cool-shamed himself out of relevance. What does a pagan need with a "pagan Christianity" that is simply two steps behind the most exciting parts of unfiltered paganism?

Politics

I am writing this in the time of a heated political season in the
United States. Frankly, the options that stand before us are exactly
the options we deserve as a people. That is to say, both candidates
are—how to say it? —*nincompoops*. This much can hardly be con-
tested. Neither major political party are clear champions for the
Christian worldview, but one political party is, at its base level, in
direct opposition to the Christian worldview. It is the party that
races with its own members to see who is the most radical in

socialist ideology, sexual licentiousness, and "reproductive healthcare"—which has to be the most brazen and ironic manifestations of newspeak to date. It takes a truly active imagination to take a term like "abortion"—already a euphemism for "hacking up an unborn baby in his or her mother's womb"—and calling it "healthcare."

So, while the exact course of actions may not be clear for the Christian in a democratic election, it should be obvious that certain options are *not on the table*. Like, for example, the party that obsesses over the "right" to kill babies. You would think it would be obvious that the Christian should not cast his ballot for the pro-baby-killing party. Yet, to assume such would be to vastly underestimate the power of cool-shaming. When the pro-baby-killing party is deemed the party of the cool, all manner of mental gymnastics become possible, nay, *necessary*. Suddenly, what appeared black and white morphs into a greyish blob, and you are no longer faced with the party that is often hypocritical on the one hand, and the party that insists on killing babies on the other, but rather two equally flawed parties that are equally good in some respects. "Sure, the party on the right may be pro-life in the sense that it insists upon not killing babies, but the party on the left is pro-life in the sense that it doesn't like the death penalty. Same thing, right?"

This kind of disproportionate reasoning eventually leads not merely to unbalanced judgments, but directly lopsided judgments. Before long, the prospective voter is insisting that, contrary to the laws of logic and common sense, you actually get less of what you *subsidize* and more of what you *penalize*, and therefore that voting for the pro-baby-killing party will actually get you, by some miracle, less babies killed.

Now, this does not mean that the Christian *must* vote for the other side—the side that ostensibly does not prefer killing babies. There may be many good reasons not to vote for a party, but included in that number of good reasons is not the ability to *get to say you didn't vote that way.* It is not a good reason to vote one way purely out of an attempt to distance yourself from those who voted the other way as a tactic to impress them. That actually won't earn street cred for the pagan who is not satisfied with knowing that you did not simply vote for the *wrong* party, but that you positively enthused about the *right* party (which is definitely not the party on the right). To be cool-shamed is to be backed into a corner willingly; the cool-shamed Christian is not a prisoner of war, he is a voluntary slave. And the one chasing after the attention of pagan society does not realize that what he does will never be enough. The goal post changes constantly.

But the greatest need to avoid being cool-shamed is not how unbecoming and embarrassing it looks. It is that to be cool-shamed is to commit a grave sin against God. It is to fear man over fearing God. Many of us are aware of what Paul says in Romans 1:18–31 for the most part, but the final phrase of the final verse does not get nearly enough press. "Though they know God's righteous decree that those who practice such things deserve to die, they not only do them *but give approval to those who practice them.*"

According to Paul, sin is manifested not only in certain actions, but also in the *approval of certain actions.* This should be taken as a stark warning for those with that insatiable craving for the high opinions of others. Those of us whose *worse nightmare* is being labeled a bigot, or close-minded, or prudish. In a godless society, there is no reconciling "cool" with "Christian." We can fool ourselves into thinking that our incessant man-fearing amounts to "maintaining a good witness," when it is actually straightforward worldliness.

It is not enough to *technically* disapprove of what Scripture defines as sin, but function as if one were not bothered by them. And while this does not mean that we should walk around with signs and assume a posture of vitriol and self-righteous malice, it does mean that the sin in our society should *grieve us.*

To put the matter directly, our lost neighbors are not helped by our obsession for their approval. "Please, think I'm cool! I'm not one of *those* crazy Christians. Ick. I'm cool. I'm one of you. I get it. Think I'm cool. Please, think I'm cool. Your sin is cool with me. I'm *technically* against it, but between you and me, I wouldn't make nearly as big of a deal about it as Paul does." That is not love of neighbor. That is mercenary; an ego-centric attempt to flatter oneself at the expense of a neighbor's persistence in sin. Instead, faithfulness would have us lament and grieve over and hate all sin, including the sin of our neighbors, not because we are in ourselves any better off, but because sin is fundamentally self-destructive, since it is against God and against nature.

Chapter 4
On Not Despising Children

Among the many disheartening features of Western culture, here at the late hour of modernity's twilight, is its general dislike of children. Marshaling evidence for dislike isn't difficult. It is safe to assume that a culture that likes children won't eradicate so many of them before they exit the womb. The body count since Roe v Wade, which is upward of sixty-two million, erases any illusions that our culture prefers the presence of children over their absence. But let us say, for the sake of argument, that this were not the case. Let us pretend, only briefly (and it should be *brief*, for we should not long forget the crime), that our Western culture wasn't in the practice of destroying the equivalence of cities and states and civilizations on a yearly basis; might we find other evidences that our culture despises children?

I confess I find all too many. One memory comes to mind of a leisurely stroll down Capitol Hill in Seattle while my wife and I were visiting some friends. Despite the fact that the City streets were peppered with the occasional raving homeless person under the influence of God-knows-what, or the occasional rainbow-clad crossdresser, the most conspicuous and starkly *strange* sight on that day was the four offspring under the age of five, whom we pushed around on strollers (those rare and exotic contraptions so foreign to that region of the world). This does not in itself denote a culture-wide dislike for children. But the number of restaurants decorated with signs that read, "No Children Allowed," could hardly communicate such a sentiment any more emphatically. It was an exciting change for my children to be in a place where dogs greatly outnumbered little people like them, but this was only exciting because they could not interpret this as the statement the city was in fact making to them: *we don't want you. We don't like you. We prefer life without you.*

Speaking of dogs, I wonder if "man's best friend" might also teach us about our culture's dislike of children. Not directly, of course, but indirectly. Humans have always loved dogs, but what is happening today seems unique. In an "identity age," where most people are driven by the assumption that identity is not inherited, but self-wrought (thanks a lot, Sartre and godless existentialism), people are obsessed with "identifying" themselves with certain markers. I understand it is common to flag these markers in the "bio" section of social media accounts. Increasingly common is the identity marker of "dog mom," diligently raising her "fur babies."

There is, of course, a spectrum of seriousness with this sort of thing. Some sport their bumper-stickers tongue-in-cheek. This would be harmless, and even *cute*, were it not for the many who do not in the least exaggerate when they speak thusly about their pets (we should hasten to add that such a person would be aghast at my use of the word "pet" to describe their furry family member).

Again, this might not mean a lot by itself, but it certainly fits much more in a culture that despises children than one that treasures them—it makes sense for an elevated value of pets to coincide with a depreciating value of children. And this kind of—let us call it—*idoglatry* certainly harmonizes with an ever-growing secularization, where man is nothing more than matter-in-motion, just like everything else. Combine this metaphysic with an unprecedented self-obsession and you have the perfect storm for idoglatry: why bear children when you can simply have a fur-baby? If the only thing tiny creatures are good for is fulfilling one's own desire for companionship, why have the kind that requires grueling levels of self-sacrifice? The sad twist of irony is that such a cost-benefit analysis, in the end, deprives such people not only of their human usefulness, or the joy of child-bearing, but it in fact impoverishes them of the pure joy of owning a pet. This, as C.S. Lewis pointed out, is what occurs when second things assume the place of first things: "The woman who makes a dog the center of her life loses, in the end, not only her human usefulness and dignity but even the proper pleasure of dog-keeping."[1]

But here I have gotten ahead of myself. I've moved on to consider an implicit evidence of cultural child-dislike when there are still explicit examples. Examples like Sarah Le Marquand who argues that being a stay-at-home mother should be illegal.[2] She reasons that such women are leaches on the society, feeding on the economy while producing nothing (save the future men and women who will maintain the economy in a few short decades, whose success or failure will be determined, in large part, by the way such women raise them—this doesn't seem to outweigh the cost of the bottom dollar, for Marquand).

Absent from this reasoning is any concern for the children, whom Marquand seems eager to de-mother for the common good. But if pressed on the point, she might find sanctuary in a reason academic journal article published by Elizabeth Bartholet,[3] in which she argues that homeschooling ought to be illegal since it creates the possibility of children inheriting ideas that dissent from "ideas and values central to our democracy." We might say that Bartholet objects to parents brainwashing their children on the grounds that it prevents the state from doing so.

Where Marquand wants to protect society from mothers, Bartholet wants to protect children from mothers. In the case, it is

---

[1] C.S. Lewis, "First and Second Things," in *God in the Dock: Essays in Theology and Culture* (Grand Rapids: MI, Eerdmans, 2014).

[2] "It should be illegal to be a stay-at-home mum," *The Daily Telegraph* (Published on March 21, 2017. https://www.dailytelegraph.com.au/rendezview/sarrah-le-marquand-it-should-be-illegal-to-be-a-stayathome-mum/news-story/fbd6fe7b79e8b4136 d49d991b6a1f41c. Accessed on November 3, 2020).

[3] Elizabeth Bartholet, "Homeschooling: Parent Rights Absolutism vs. Child Rights Education & Protection" in *The Arizona Law Review*, vol. 61, issue 1, 2020.

difficult to distinguish the chicken from the egg: is a totalitarian conception of state-children relationship the cause of an increasing antipathy and dislike for children, or vice versa? Either way, the net result is that children are not valued as human-beings, but rather as aids or obstacles to a secular project.

It is not likely such expressions of dislike will be present in most churches, but the residual effects of a culture that dislikes children are felt in churches all too often. Consider, for example, the hard separation most evangelicals take for granted between sex and child-bearing. This is certainly an improvement from the wider culture, which makes another hard separation between marriage and sex (most evangelicals have not gone that far, at least not on paper), but to insist that the topic of marital sexual expression and child-bearing in marriage are two unrelated questions, and *never the twain shall meet*, is to tear asunder what God has joined together. This leads to the kind of heartbreaking scene all too familiar to fruitful Christian couples, when their "We are expecting *again!*" is met with blank stairs and bepuzzlement. "But… *why?*" A great response to that question might sound something like, "Because we are not fools. Because we know what gifts are, and we prefer to receive them with gratitude, thank you."

> Behold, children are a heritage from the LORD,
>   the fruit of the womb a reward.
> Like arrows in the hand of a warrior
>   are the children of one's youth.
> Blessed is the man
>   who fills his quiver with them!
> He shall not be put to shame
>   when he speaks with his enemies in the gate (Ps. 127:3–5).

What warrior prefers fewer quivers in his arrow to more? When God offers a gift, "What makes it so special?" is never the appropriate response. When God offers a gift, you receive it, and say "Thank you." The kind of ingratitude that develops a *dislike* for the God-given treasure of children is not only a slap in the face to those who desperately *long for* that treasure (i.e., those who are burdened with infertility), or those who desperately *miss* that treasure (i.e., those who have experienced the loss of miscarriage or the death of a child), it is also self-impoverishing. As is often the case, this last point has been made better, and more effectively, by G.K. Chesterton. We close with his reflections on the irony of those who object to child-bearing on the grounds that they insist on maintaining "freedom:"

> Now a child is the very sign and sacrament of personal freedom. He is a fresh free will added to the wills of the world; he is something that his parents have freely chosen to produce and which they freely agree to protect. They can feel that any amusement he gives (which is often considerable) really comes from him and from them, and from nobody else… He is a creation and a contribution; he is their own creative contribution to creation. He is also a much more beautiful, wonderful, amusing, and astonishing thing than any of the stale stories or jingling jazz tunes turned out by the machines. When men no longer feel that he is so, they have lost the appreciation of primary things, and therefore all sense of proportion about the world. People who prefer the mechanical pleasures, to such a miracle, are jaded and enslaved. They are preferring the very dregs of life to the first fountains of life. They are preferring the last, crooked, indirect, borrowed, repeated, and exhausted things of our dying Capitalist civilization, to the reality which is the only rejuvenation of all civilization. It is they who are hugging the chains of their old slavery; it is the child who is ready for the new world.[4]

---

[4] G.K. Chesterton, "Babies and Distribution" in *In Defense of Sanity: The Best Essay of G.K. Chesterton* (San Francisco, CA: Saint Ignatius Press, 2011), 272–273.

Chapter 5
Envy at Seminary

If I have seen it once, I have seen it a thousand times. A fresh seminarian, wide-eyed and hungry for knowledge, steps onto campus and, within the first semester, finds himself in the throes of full-blown battle with a litany of subtle sins for which no one prepared him. Of course, he was warned of many dangers. He was warned, "Don't be so heavenly-minded that you're no earthly good," and, even though he had C.S. Lewis in his corner correcting the misconception, the kernel of truth had taken root: "Don't forget about the people; this is all for the Church—it can't stay forever theoretical." *Check.* He was warned, "Beware of the temptation to allow your theological studies to become purely academic: remember to make it worship." *Check.* He was warned, "Don't put your personal prayer and Scripture intake on the backburner; a Church History textbook is no replacement for humble and quiet soul-feeding." *Check.*

But *no one* warned him, "Beware of envy." No one warned him of this single, most dangerous and formidable of foes, who swallows up unsuspecting victims in a single gulp. It prowls in every class and every online interaction and every after-class conversation, and *no one*—not one single person—warned him!

If I sound incredulous it's because I am—this one is personal. The deep struggle with this sin was something for which I was not remotely prepared. And as a pastor of a church neighboring an evangelical seminary, I have a front-row view of this hidden trapdoor. For years I've watched student after student fall into the snare, unawares. So, with this essay, hear me saying, "Be careful! There's a trap right *there.*"

"Envy" may seem like a counterintuitive sin to warn incoming seminarians about, but it has proven a true enough opponent by both personal experience and observation. Most of the time, this nasty little sin doesn't show its ugly face outright. It wears a smile. But you can tell when it's there by the odd behavior it induces. For example, all the "humble brags" on social media have a green shade if you look closely enough. *"So blessed to have all these publications added to my resume!" "So humbled to have my name in this prof's book as a research assistant." "Hey super-awesome professor, thanks for that private conversation we just had in your office where you told me how much promise I have. Totally not tweeting this out just to let the world know you and I are close. #Blessed."*

You may be surprised by the suggestion that envy is behind these kinds of shenanigans, but hear me out. Envy can really be understood as "pride *next to people.*" That is, the manifestation of your pride when you start looking to your right and to your left with a measuring stick. As far as I can tell, there are at least three outcomes for this game of comparison.

Self-aggrandizement, Self-promotion, Self-advancement
The first is self-aggrandizement. Self-promotion. Self-advancement. This manifestation of envy is perhaps the hardest to spot in yourself and the easiest to spot in others. The euphemistic word for it is *ambition.* But a more accurate word for it is *slimy.* It is that hunger for recognition. C.S. Lewis identifies this as the pull of the *Inner Ring.* He says,

> The lust for the esoteric, the longing to be inside, take many forms which are not easily recognizable as Ambition. We hope, no doubt, for tangible profits from every Inner Ring we penetrate: power, money, liberty to break rules... But all these would not satisfy us if we did not get in addition the delicious sense of secret intimacy... Unless you take measures to prevent it, this desire is going to be one of the chief motives of your life, from

the first day on which you enter your profession until the day when you are too old to care.[1]

There are at least a couple reasons this is so dangerous. First of all, it misses the entire point of what seminaries are for: the glory of *God*. The envious seminary student who constantly promotes himself is the anti-John the Baptist. He says, "Jesus must decrease, I must increase." He's the friend of the bridegroom who shows up at the wedding and, rather than rejoicing at the sound of his best mate saying, "I do," tries to get the attention of the bride for *himself* (Jn. 3:22–36). That is what most our *platform-building* amounts to. "No, no, I'm doing it *for the gospel*," objects the self-promoter. And this is why it's so hard to get a hold of this thing; it's covered in oil and slips through our grasp. It is easy to rebrand it as something honorable. But it is what it is. We aren't doing ourselves any favors by trying to spin our self-aggrandizement as anything but dishonoring to God. A fellow pastor and friend of mine once said it like this, "Make sure you don't pass by Jesus on his path of descent while you're trying to make a name for yourself."[2]

The second reason self-aggrandizement is dangerous can be summed up like this: you can't become what you insist you are already are. If you promote yourself as the well-accomplished genius you want to be known as, you will find it hard to humble yourself and take on the posture of *an actual student*. To the degree you believe your reputation is established you will hesitate to ask questions and seek clarification. Someone makes a comment about an obscure theological concept and assumes you know what she's talking about. You feel flattered that, in her mind, you are informed on such matters. Except in this case you're not. Do you

[1] C.S. Lewis, "The Inner Ring" in *The Weight of Glory* (New York, NY: HarperOne, 2001), 151–152.
[2] Ronni Kurtz, in an unrecorded sermon.

"out" yourself as ignorant? "Wait, I've never heard of that, could you explain yourself?" That's what a humble learner would do. Or do you let the flattery work its way through your head and out your mouth? "Ah yes, of course. Astute observation." That is a learning opportunity squandered.

Resentment

The second outcome of uncontested envy is resentment. Inevitably, when you look to your left and to your right, *someone* will be standing higher than you. Someone will have the attention you want from a certain professor. Someone will receive an opportunity you desire. If envy sets in, you will find yourself unable to rejoice with them or for them. You will find yourself pouting. Whatever reason you previously had for self-congratulations just feels small now. Discontentment spreads, and the accomplishments of your friends begin to feel like personal injuries. "This is a zero-sum game: an opportunity they get is an opportunity I miss."

I distinctly remember when this became real for me. A friend of mine published an article on a topic I was passionate about, and on which I had written a great deal. The article was a big hit, and I agreed with everything in it. It was a *biblical* article, just like—I pray—mine were. And the effects his article had were what I primarily wanted (or at least, what I *believed* I wanted) out of my articles on the topic. People found these ideas helpful. Great, right? As it turns out, my desires for these ideas to glorify God and serve his people were not as pure as I once thought. I couldn't celebrate the fact that people were helped by the article because it wasn't *my* article. "He must increase… but *must I decrease? How come my friend gets to increase a little?*" (cf., Jn. 21:21).

Despair

The third fruit of envy after it has had its way is despair. This is the self-loathing turn. Envy turns the soul sour, especially when it turns introspective. This happens when we look to our left and right and count the accomplishments or intellectual abilities or level of personal piety of brothers and sisters around us, and then take that measurement and stand underneath it. As we look up, the distance between our status and their towering achievement crushes the soul. *I'm so far behind. I'll never catch up. I'll never have his clarity of thought. I'll never have her systematic theological knowledge. I'll never preach like him.*

Often, when we see this in ourselves or others, we think we need to be coddled. *Someone tell me how special I am! Tell me I'm wrong about this low view of myself and that I am the greatest thing to happen to the Church since John Piper!* No. What we really need is good ole fashioned rebuke. Don't be deceived, this is envy. It is prideful self-importance. Such a one need not be coddled back to self-esteem and told that he actually does measure up, because the *measuring* is the problem. How one measures up to the people next to oneself is simply not the point. Prideful self-aggrandizement and insecure self-loathing are two sides of the same coin. Insecurity is still pride, it is just what pride looks like all bruised up.

So, we ought to add this warning to the current list of sins students are on the lookout for: beware of envy. The seminary environment is unavoidably good soil for it to grow, so we should be vigilant and rip it out. Confess it. Forsake it. Put it to death. The potential for rich fruit in this season of life is too important to allow this thistle of envy to choke it out.

Chapter 6
Engaging the Culture
(with Carl F.H. Henry)

"No society can long take a rain check on final commitments."
Carl F.H. Henry

A generation of evangelicals feel homeless, in more ways than one. News stories report on what evangelicalism is responsible for, what evangelicals value, how they think, what they live for, and my friends and I look at one another and struggle to find in our own ranks any resemblance. This presses us into very odd behavior indeed.

On the one hand, we feel tempted to throw our hands in the air and despair of any social, political, cultural engagement at all. "We will not be cast accurately anyway," some of us think, "what's the point?" Others of us decide that what we need most is to nuance our way out of the extreme Right, while remaining Right enough to be Christian. So we clamor for the attention of secularists and say, "Yeah, *those* MAGA hat-sporting evangelicals *really are the worst*. I'm not like that, though. I'm one of the cool Christians. Yes, *technically* I'm complementarian, but between you and me, I'm not all that happy about Paul's restrictions on women preachers; let me tell you about all the loopholes I found." And in both of these extremes, politics-by-Twitter has produced that deadly combination of throbbing political arrogance and drooling political ignorance.

Some of us are aware of both these errors but still wonder what a faithful evangelicalism looks like. We want an evangelicalism that is theologically grounded. We want an evangelicalism that avoids escapism and isn't afraid of politics. We want an evangelicalism that isn't idolatrous, and that declines the chalice of social power by any means necessary. We want an evangelicalism that is uniquely Christian, and not bi-partisan. We want an evangelicalism that isn't so fragile that it cannot identify real injustice or societal sins on the one hand, and isn't willing to parrot anti-Christian ideologies to diagnose and resolve those injustices on the other. We want an evangelicalism that helps us thread the needle of being citizens of heaven and sojourners on earth.

Enter Carl F. H. Henry. The kind of evangelicalism we want is the kind Henry helped to build. In terms of our political, social, cultural moment, here's the biggest lesson Henry teaches us: *common grace demands Christian concern for the common good. But common grace also commands the Christian reject the "common ground" delusion.*[1] "Common grace" and "common ground" are different. For example, what does the gospel have to do with the amalgam of Marxism and Intersectionality and Postmodernism in terms of partnership? Nothing. The cosmology the former assumes differs fundamentally from that of the latter. They stand on differing *grounds*.

Yet, this does not mean that the Christian must eschew the woke secularist's social concerns as imaginary. Some Christians have concluded that since biblical Christianity and neo-Marxism share nothing by way of philosophical foundations, they must share nothing by way of observation. So they hear some talk of institutionalized racism, or systemic injustice, and they say, "Hogwash, they are imagining things." But seeing a problem and diagnosing it are two very different things.

You don't have to be "woke" to know that red-lining was a *sin* that has scarred many minority communities. Sins tend to have a chain reaction, and it is not at all inconsistent to say that a young black man is sinning for assaulting a police officer on the one

---

[1] By calling "common ground" a delusion, I am not here rejecting what I affirmed in chapter 1; namely, the doctrine of "common notions." See pg. 4 note 1.

hand, and insisting that his sin may have been incentivized by a complex of sins committed *against him* that affected him his whole life on the other—like the sins of commoditizing police work to pad the pockets of state magistrates, or the sin of obscuring justice by locking up an entire generation of fathers like animals in a cage and calling it "rehabilitation" for crimes that should have simply been penalized or punished with just proportion, etc. Pointing the finger at fatherlessness is all well and good and judicious, but fatherlessness has a complex of causes, including subsidized de-fathering—let's point the finger at that too, shall we?

What were we talking about again? Right. Henry.

Few public theologians have demonstrated the kind of precision needed better than Carl F. H. Henry. It would be very easy to find one-off lines from Henry and marshal him as the ally of a particular tribe. To those "don't talk about social injustice, just preach the gospel" types, the other side could appeal to Henry in their defense: "Hence a sharp and costly disjunction arose, whereby many evangelicals made the mistake of relying on evangelism alone to preserve world order and many liberals made the mistake of relying wholly on socio-political action to solve world problems."[2] Or again: "The Christian has social duties not simply as a Christian but as a man, and his sanctification therein does not come about automatically without pulpit instruction in sound scriptural principles."[3] Or again: "Despite the perils, no evasion of responsibility for meaningfully relating the gospel to the pressing problems of modern life is tolerable."[4] Or again: "By such evangelical Protestant evasion of the larger problems of social justice… contemporary evangelicals contrast sharply with their Reformation heritage."[5] Henry is not at all content with Christians

---

[2] Carl F.H. Henry, *Architect of Evangelicalism: Essential Essays of Carl F.H. Henry* (Bellingham, WA: Lexham Press, 2019), 44.

[3] Henry, *Architect of Evangelicalism*, 45–46.

[4] Henry, *Architect of Evangelicalism*, 20.

[5] Henry, *Architect of Evangelicalism*, 287.

taking a raincheck on cultural engagement. No, they may not see themselves out of conversations about societal justice, says Henry, for they are to love their neighbor.

And yet, after firing off at the social justice naysayers, he can turn right around to offer a few choice words to "woke" Christians as well. "If evangelical conscience is to be a remedial and transforming social force, then evangelical convictions require articulate mobilization *on their own account*,"[6] not on the account of secular theories, for example. Or again: "To write Christian theology in terms of *any* culture-orientation is hazardous."[7] Or again: "How may [socialism] be introduced most compellingly [to the Church]? By stressing that poverty is obviously an evil, and by citing cases of destitution that—in the *post*-Christian era—would stir even a pagan conscience. Next, churches are called to condemn, not only the misuse of riches and the exploitation and neglect of the poor, *but the very idea of economic disproportion.* The clergy are urged to badger the wealthy into sharing their possessions voluntarily with the poor, or to promote the multiplication of their tax burdens as a means of involuntary equalization."[8] Or again: "That the growing government monopoly of welfare activity is hailed as a valid expression of Christian love for neighbor… calls for earnest soul-searching. *The Church will always pay a high price for giving to Caesar what belongs to God.*"[9]

In the end, no one walks away from Henry unscathed. He pins every one of us to the floor. Simply put, Carl F. H. Henry is one of the greatest theological minds the American Baptists have ever known. He was a public theologian and a public intellectual. He read widely. He saw the relevance of Christ's lordship on every topic he came across, and then he wrote about it in cogent and

---

[6] Henry, *Architect of Evangelicalism*, 45.
[7] Henry, *Architect of Evangelicalism*, 201.
[8] Henry, *Architect of Evangelicalism*, 306.
[9] Henry, *Architect of Evangelicalism*, 319.

winsome fashion. But what separates him from a handful of other notable Baptist public intellectuals is his *depth*. One might imagine such breadth in one figure would mean his limitations on mastery, until one stumbles upon his six-volume project, *God, Revelation, and Authority*. In his career, Henry demonstrated both breadth and depth.

And also *pithiness*. The man could turn a phrase. Casually reading Henry is difficult, because he arrests his reader's attention with phrases like, "Man is made for God, and without God he is not wholly man; the godless myths hold promise only for the making of monsters;"[10] or "An American classroom that yields irreligious students, and ignores the facts of the Hebrew-Christian religion and its heritage, is neither the friend of democracy nor the foe of totalitarianism;"[11] or "Any generation that prices intercourse above all other intimacies and thinks that through physical love alone, apart from any transcendent relationship, the sex act unlocks life's deepest secrets and exhausts its mysteries, is doomed to deadly superficiality."[12] *Oh Henry, if you could only see us now.*

Of course, Henry was by no means perfect. Like every theologian East of Eden, he had massive blind spots—blind spots we should not dismiss too lightly, especially since some of them were not shared by his own contemporaries. An example would be his views on abortion. While he identified broadly with pro-life sentiments, he nevertheless published some pretty horrifying words on the issue of abortion and the *imago Dei*.[13] Indeed, that part of Henry's corpus is, in my estimation, the single greatest tragedy and disappointment of his career. But while this does not excuse

---

[10] Henry, *Architect of Evangelicalism*, 161.

[11] Henry, *Architect of Evangelicalism*, 226.

[12] Henry, *Architect of Evangelicalism*, 322.

[13] Henry writes, "When childbirth would endanger the mother's life abortion can be morally justifiable. The fetus seems less than human, moreover, in cases of extreme deformity in which rational and moral capacities integral to the imago Dei are clearly lacking." Carl F.H. Henry, *The Christian Mindset in a Secular Society: Promoting Evangelical Renewal & National Righteousness* (Portland: Multnomah Press, 1984), 103.

such words as he published, it should be noted that these sentiments are aberrations of an otherwise faithful career in public theology. Henry managed to publish such thoughts *despite* his con-
sistency of thought as a public theologian, not because of it. All in
all, I commend the writings of Carl F. H. Henry to anyone concerned with faith in the public square; he has much to teach us if
we would but listen. The Lord knows the Baptist world is aching
for the kind of precision our older brother Henry so faithfully
demonstrated. Let us follow his example.

Chapter 7
My Departure from Social Media

Recently, I joined the exclusive and burgeoning millennial mo-
nastic order of *Socialis Instrumentis Refugatus* (the order of the
Social Media Refugee). I live in the technological wilderness,
where I forget about birthdays and require verbal summaries from
friends and family about what the Donald is up to.[1] Now, before
you fall over from sheer amazement at my staggering piety, allow
me to disabuse you of the notion that this departure is somehow
a feat of grand ascetic accomplishment. I did not forsake social
media because I am teeming with self-disciplinary strength. Quite
the opposite, in fact. You see, I am far too weak for social media.
Since I do not want to get in the habit of despising any common
grace instruments handed down from our heavenly Father, or
shirking the stewardship of wealth (in this instance, technological
wealth), I hope to build up some resilience and one day re-enter
the fray.[2]

And this is why I have no problem with the fact that you, my
dear reader, probably found out about this book online—on social
media. To this day, the spread of my writing depends in large part
on the press I get from *others on social media*. Our exchange right
now, therefore, between the author and the reader, is one of a confession from a weaker brother to a stronger brother or sister. You
may have the fortitude that I lack to occupy space online whilst
maintaining a soul. In that case, you have my respect. (It is also

---

[1] Here, I am referring to the United States' 45th president, Donald J. Trump, who
is sometimes affectionately (and sometimes not so affectionately) nicknamed "the
Donald."

[2] By the time you are holding this book, this aforesaid day will have come. Pray for
me.

possible that you are a weakling like me, listening in on this confession to the strong. If you find yourself identifying with my infirmities and decide that you too are in need of a holiday in the wilderness, *Socialis Instrumentis Refugatus* has room for you). The social media detox is taking time, however, which is why my **weaknesses will be itemized in bold; in true tweetable, skimmable, bloggable form.** I have not yet kicked the habit of writing for the reader on the go, in a hurry to plumb deeper into the bottomless ocean of the *feed*. I have left social media for the following four reasons.

I am far too vain

This is in truth the chief reason for why I *had* to leave social media, and the chief reason I had such a hard time doing it. You must understand—and I must ask you to refrain from scoffing at what I'm about to say—I love to write. In fact, I'd like to *become* a writer someday (still not really sure when I am allowed to claim that title). Now, I already have several obstacles in the way of this dream. First of all, I am, for whatever reason, quite slow to heed the council of my betters when writing.[3] For one so handicapped as is, I'm not doing myself any favors in the realm of publication by leaving social media. Publishers, I am told, like to see that inquiring authors have a following on social media. They like to see their authors active in self-promotion and such, and for good reason. Publishing groups, after all, are businesses, and authors are makers of the products those businesses push. They want to see that the investment of a publication is a good one; one that promises a fruitful return.

I don't despise this reality at all. What I despise is my own lust for praise. My egomaniacal desire for "platform." The way my heart warms at the fire emoji responses to my articles. The shares.

---

[3] Like Jason Duesing, who—if reading this—has surely lost count of my adverbs. Kindly forgive me, Jason.

The retweets. The likes. It's all just far too delicious. I am an addict on the road to recovery.

I am too prone to overreact with cynicism or sentimentalism
The former is fed by, and expressed in, the snark. The cheap sarcasm. The dehumanization. The dismissive meme at the expense of "*them.*" The lazy, uncritical, uncareful trolling. My wife once read me a Facebook comment that read somewhere along the lines of, "If your *@#$! kid invades my dog's space I'm glad if she bites him! My dog's feelings are no less important than your snotty little kid's." I am capable of responding to such tomfoolery with a number of reactions, but one that is all too often missing from my reservoir is a cool-headed application of Proverbs 26:4-5. I simply do not have the self-control of keeping myself from cynicism.

Or sentimentalism, for that matter. This is the pendulum's other side, which is showing up in dramatic fashion now that we've experienced years of its counterpart. Once we despair of cynicism, we react with a form of "if you don't got noth'n nice to say, don't say noth'n at all," which often transforms into, "if there's noth'n nice to say, make someth'n up." Before leaving social media, I saw this in the form of cool-cat evangelicals expressing how much they missed Obama's presidential decorum ("sure he was religiously committed to making infanticide widespread, but look how well-spoken he was!"). If you're wondering if sentimentalism has crept into your social media feed, do a word search for "nuance" and see if any straightforwardly dividing question has been gagged and bound and nuanced to death.

The overreaction against cynicism to sentimentalism compels Christians on social media to disqualify satire or criticism or public rebuke wholesale. But if we adopt that principle, we will have a hard time with Paul's "tone" in 2 Corinthians 11, where he essentially puts on the mask of a "super-apostle" and then acts like the fool. "Look at me, I'm a *'super*-apostle.'" He does this so as to expose how embarrassingly dumb his opponents look, and how embarrassingly dumb the Corinthians look for being dazzled by them. The whole chapter is impossible to make sense of unless you read it with a sarcastic tone of voice. Or Galatians 5:12, where Paul challenges the Judaizing influence in the Church of Galatia. They were harassing the Gentile believing men in Galatia to circumcise themselves and keep the Law of Moses if they wanted to *really* be included in the family of God. So Paul says that those who were so obsessed with circumcision should take their zeal to the next level. Don't stop at circumcision, go all the way! "I wish they would practice circumcision 2.0 and just cut off their..." *Paul, Paul, Paul, think about your witness! The world doesn't need any more harshness. Be a tad bit more nuanced in your response to these men.*

I am too tribalistic

This is one of those self-discoveries of my own weakness that didn't show up until after I left social media. It was an issue I was aware of *in principle* before I left, but it was a bit like a fish knowing the principle of "wetness," having nothing to contrast it with. It's a special kind of fear of man that *postures* you toward agreeing with one party and disagreeing with another before considering the topic on its own terms.

> *What do we believe again?*
> *What's my line?*
> *He just made a pretty good point...But let me check to see what so-and-so has to say before I know if I can agree with him or not.*

Having trusted voices to consult is a good thing, but I have found my time on social media fosters something far more extreme and far more insidious. This kind of tribalism marks the beginning of the end of intellectual honesty, and with it, the end of meaningful discourse. If there's no room for challenging the party line in any way, the tribe we live in is less of a family and more of a totalitarian group-think. When this is present, cancel culture is not long behind (more on this in chapter thirteen).

I am too undisciplined with my time

"I don't have enough time in the day," I tweet, after ten minutes of mindlessly scrolling and before ten more. Before I left social media, I was prone to lament my anxiety and stress and fidgety disposition, while remaining completely unwilling to limit my time on social media. This is ironic because there is now no question at all about the adverse sociological and psychological effects of social media overuse. The science is conclusive: spending too much time there really does increase your stress, anxiety, and depression.[4] This is why, at the time I am writing this, our iPhones now have the capability to set time limits on our apps. This is a wonderful thing, but when all is said and done, it must be coupled with the level of self-discipline required for declining the "15 more minutes" offer—a level of self-discipline this millennial monk clearly lacks.

Ultimately, self-discipline is all about what you value. Because I valued that jolt of dopamine you get from checking for "notifications" above having three minutes of uninterrupted contemplation, I was squandering my time. I find now that I don't really lament my lack of minutes, because instead of watching them sink into Instagram stories, I am busy enjoying them with G.K. Chesterton. When you find yourself in a midday lull with several minutes to spend between tasks, just remember: the cost of

---

[4] This address by Felicia Wu Song is particularly enlightening and disturbing in this regard: "Digital Life as Secular Liturgy," *The Center for Pastor Theologians* (Published on November 11, 1919. https://www.pastortheologians.com/podcasthomepage-/2019/10/14/cpt-podcast-episode-34. Accessed, November 3, 2020).

minutes it takes to work through your notifications can also buy you a Chesterton essay entitled "What I Found in My Pocket." Before waving away such an essay as just as big a waste of time as a cat video, know that such a judgment would make you miss out on sentences like these:

> Now I deny most energetically that anything is, or can be, uninteresting. So I stared at the joints of the walls and seats, and began thinking hard on the fascinating subject of wood. Just as I had begun to realize why, perhaps, it was that Christ was a carpenter, rather than a bricklayer, or a baker, or anything else, I suddenly started upright, and remembered my pockets.[5]

I rest my case. One day, "@Samuel_Parkison" may return to twitter, to begin the rewarding labor of acquiring followers once again. But because of the aforementioned deficiencies, I think you'll agree it's better that day doesn't arrive anytime soon. For now, the wilderness suits me. *Selah.*

---

[5] G.K. Chesterton, "What I Found in My Pocket" in *In Defense of Sanity,* 36–37.

Chapter 8

Entertainment
(and the Self-Deception of a "Strong Conscience")

Imagine the scene with me for a moment, if you would. You're standing with a group of friends, and someone makes an obscure reference to *The Office*. You get the reference, and acknowledge your familiarity with a chuckle. Then you see your friend's reference and raise him one. Now you're off to the races. Before long, several minutes pass by in laughter and direct quotes and descriptions.

I have watched—and participated in—this scene by appreciators of *The Office* (of whom I am the foremost) more times than I can count. For the most part, it is pretty innocuous. Most often, the humor we celebrate is the essential humor of the show: the comic reality of the awkward. At its best, this kind of humor teaches us to be the kind of people who don't take ourselves seriously, and that is a good thing. If we can come to think of our foibles and serendipitous mistakes (like spilling over an *entire* pot of chili and then slipping all over it, for example) as the punchline to a joke—ourselves being the faithful characters of a brilliant comedy Writer—we will be the better for it.

But suppose at the end of a *really long* TV quote-a-thon, you notice one friend uncomfortably looking at his shoes, waiting for the whole thing to conclude. You ask him if he watches *The Office* and he says no. Upon your pressing and prodding, he reluctantly gives you his rationale: "I have a really addictive personality, and it's hard for me to watch TV without watching it in excess. Besides, I've watched a couple of episodes and the humor seems to me to be in bad taste. I just don't think it would do much to increase my affections for Christ." What's your response in that scenario? Apart from the agonizing desire to lighten the mood, to which your friend just added unbearable poundage, you may feel a bit of admiration for his zeal. You may even feel a little bit of— dare I say—*conviction.*

But then you don't, because *wait just a minute!* Isn't this a conscience issue? And what about that very spiritual, redemptive paragraph I just wrote about not taking yourself so seriously? And you don't watch the show in excess like your friend is prone to do. And "common grace" and what not. And to each his own. And your conscience just isn't as tender as this poor brother. And before long, you are assuaging your conscience and feeling piously sorry for your friend who is enslaved to his legalistic tendencies.

Ok, this internal self-defensiveness may be an exaggeration. But suppose the scenario is slightly different. Suppose this non-TV-watching friend comes over to borrow a power-drill while you're watching TV. Suppose also he comes back two hours later and finds you exactly where he left you (five episodes deeper into the season of whatever you were watching). Suppose then that this friend, days later, asks you about the Netflix binge he interrupted, and tells you—with a furrowed brow and a somber voice—of his concern. What then? Hold that thought.

Last scenario. Suppose you are analyzing the most recent Hollywood blockbuster with *another* group of friends. Let's say it's a really potent artifact of social commentary, with profound redemptive themes. And yes, it has some tawdry sex scenes, but they exist within a story-arch that exposes the *vanity* of sexual licentiousness, so at the end of the day, they are truth-telling pieces of a realistic and redemptive story. Suppose there's another friend politely nodding, waiting for the conversation to transition into something of relevance to her. You ask her if she's seen the movie, and she says no.

No problem, you think. You love the movie so much that you suggest the group go watch it again *right now*! She declines, saying something about demands at home. Except you happen to know that she made plans to spend the afternoon with you and your friends, so upon your urging, she surrenders up her explanation: "That movie sounds pretty interesting, but I just don't like the idea of spending money to watch actors pretend to fornicate." *Didn't she just hear what I had to say?* you think. You assure her that the movie's conclusion actually vindicates her objection, and that she just needs to appreciate it as a whole—a stand-alone work of art. "I understand," she says, "but if I were an actress, I would never feel right about exposing my nakedness—intended for my husband and no other—to a camera. I don't want to be entertained by watching others do what I would be rightly reproved for doing."

As difficult to believe as it may seem right now, I have no desire whatever to start a modern pharisaical movement within the ranks of Reformed Evangelicalism. I merely suggest that we haven't thought as carefully or critically about how we consume entertainment as we ought. The standard-fare script for "culturally engaging" Christians on this topic is to place the entire conversation within the context of "conscience." So, we go to Romans 14. We talk about meat. We talk about not stumbling the weaker brother. And we resolve not to crack *The Office* jokes around some, or talk about movies with nudity around others. We then dust our hands off and move on, congratulating ourselves for our strong consciences.

Now, the conscience is most certainly relevant in this discussion. And it is entirely possible for tender consciences to stumble over very little objects because their legs are wobbly as is. They *must not* take in the entertainment that hurts their conscience, even if there is nothing objectively sinful about doing it. Even if their conscience is *wrong* to accuse them, and there is nothing intrinsically sinful in the act, the act would be, for them, sin. Not because "God really did say," but because they truly believe that "God really did say," and their indulgence reveals a heart postured in opposition to God. That's what a weak conscience does. So, this kind of thing happens.

But I don't think we should assume the basic suggestion (i.e., that Christians shouldn't indulge in worldly entertainment in the same way as the rest of the masses—either in sheer quantity or in content) is evidence of a weak conscience. When I was in high-school, my taste in entertainment was very different than it is now. I could stomach a lot more gutter humor, ruthless violence, and sexually explicit content than I can now without my conscience accusing me. What happened between high-school and now? What transition took place? I would like to suggest that my weakening stomach is not evidence of a weakening conscience. I don't believe that my ability in high-school to watch hours of *Family Guy* without the sting of conviction was a benchmark of spiritual maturity.

And this is just the point. *Maturity.* I think "Netflix binging" shouldn't be commonplace among evangelical Christians like it is today. And I think this, not because I am out to suck the resilience from healthy consciences like a leech. On the contrary. I want a *strong* conscience. One that is entirely in service to the lordship of King Jesus.

As we march on in the Christian life, taking every thought captive to obey Christ (2 Cor. 10:5), we will at some point come up to thoughts on entertainment. What does it look like for *those* thoughts to be taken captive to obey Christ? "Worldliness," I trust we all may grant, is a category that extends beyond fornication and illegal drugs. How far *does* it extend, though? Surely there is a worldly way of consuming entertainment. "Worldliness" in such terms must look like... *something.* If it doesn't look like indulging in entertainment with no discernable difference from the rest of the world (in terms of quantity and content, specifically), what *does it look like?*

Maybe we're fooling ourselves with all our talk of exegeting the culture. Maybe what's really happening is not cultural engagement, but just good ole fashioned cultural assimilation. Maybe we're not thinking about running our race with intensity because we are entangled by unnecessary weight (Heb. 12:1). Maybe a dogged desire to please the Lord with a critical economy of time isn't works-righteousness, but rather worshipful adoration. Maybe an insatiable thirst for Christ will create an earnestness that compels us to consume entertainment *differently.*

Or, maybe not. But I think these things are worth pondering.

Chapter 9
Of Dignity, Duels, and Social Media

By God's kind providence, I have found myself steeped in Paul's pastoral epistles as of late. These letters to Timothy and Titus have always struck me as sacred. Of course, all of Scripture is sacred, but there is a particular kind of paternal flavor to these letters that never fails to grip me; as a young pastor I imagine Paul, a spiritual father, speaking truths to me with an aged and wrinkled hand on my shoulder. There is a solemnity and a gravity that comes through in fatherly warmth. One generation passing wisdom on to the next. To be on the receiving end of this kind of transition is terrifying and exhilarating and weighty. The battalion Paul passes is not something to be trifled with.

One theme in these letters that has been of particular interest to me is "dignity." It seems that Paul is concerned with his disciples maintaining a dignified lifestyle. He desires for them to "lead a peaceful and quiet life, godly and dignified in every way" (1 Tim. 2:2). He expects for elders to manage their own households well "with all dignity" (1 Tim. 3:4). "Deacons likewise must be dignified, not double-tongued, not addicted to much wine, not greedy for dishonest gain" (1 Tim. 3:8), and female deacons[1] likewise "must be dignified, not slanders, but sober-minded, faithful in all things" (1 Tim. 3:11). And when considering those rowdy Cretans, Paul goes out of his way to make sure Titus knows to instruct older men to be "sober-minded, dignified, self-controlled, sound in faith, in love, and steadfastness" (Titus 2:2). Paul also knows that you have to practice what you preach, and so he reminds Titus to show himself in all respects "to be a model of good works,

---

[1] Or the wives of deacons, depending on how you render the word—I think they're female deacons but I don't care to argue about it here.

and in [his] teaching to show integrity, dignity" (Titus 2:7). It seems like Paul is always talking about dignity in these epistles, and even when he isn't using the word, he describes the conduct. Paul warns Timothy against undignified controversies that profit nothing (1 Tim. 6:3–16; 2 Tim. 2:14–18). He warns him against the kind of rash impulsivity and self-righteous quarrelsomeness that comes intuitively to young men (2 Tim 2:22–24). Instead, he promotes a humble fear of God—he instructs Timothy to "present [himself] to God as one approved, a worker who has no need to be ashamed, rightly handling the word of truth" (2 Tim 2:14).

All things considered, Paul paints a picture of what the ancients called *piety*. The expectation is not merely for Timothy or Titus or you or I to *do* (or avoid) this or that. The expectation is for us to be the kind of people who are upright, dependable, steadfast, godly, and dignified. The expectation is for us to not be impulsive or bombastic or desperate for attention. The dignified Christian is one who isn't titillated by gossip or slander; who isn't drawn like a moth to the flame of controversy and quarrels; who isn't flamboyant or obnoxious or unpredictable and unstable. The dignified Christian has rightly ordered affections and interests, and is not a hypocrite. This is particularly true of the dignified pastor. Between his instructions for godly living and his own life is little daylight. He recognizes, and does not begrudge, his responsibilities. He knows that certain things are expected of him, and he devotes himself to his duty in joy. He is far more concerned with what God thinks of him than how relevant he remains in the estimation of those around him. He is not fastidious about his appearance or his platform or his online persona. Or, as I heard in a recent sermon on this topic, the dignified pastor is one whose presence puts those around him at ease.

Now, granted, the picture I just painted in the above paragraph is a high one, and it could easily crush the downtrodden soul if sought after in an unhealthy and gospel-less manner. But I don't suspect that is our biggest temptation. What is interesting to me is that it seems like this picture of piety isn't sought after *at all*. We find ourselves in a culture that does not value dignity. I've noticed, for example, that ads on YouTube have become generally vulgar and unseemly. One can find quite a bit of wholesome content on the platform, but one has to endure absurd commercials that seem incapable of trafficking in anything but gutter humor in order to get it.

In our culture, we increasingly deride the aspiration of a dignified life. Such an aspiration is considered prudish and stuck up. It is stuffy and legalistic. The picture I painted in the above paragraph is as likely to be scoffed at as it is to be ignored. What we value, above anything else, is *authenticity*. Were we to meet such a dignified man as the one described above, we wouldn't buy it. We'd assume he were a phony, because in a culture that runs on "expressive individualism" (as Carl Trueman has observed),[2] self-control is just another word for "repression." To suggest, for example, that pastors should consider the way they dress as effecting their dignity—either positively or negatively—is to overstep a major cultural line. If, for example, you were to ask many a pastor if he felt his dress was dignified and appropriate, there's a pretty good chance he would answer, "I just *like* this style of clothing," as if that were an answer to your question (it's not, by the way). There are some things that just cannot be criticized. To suggest that the movies some pastors watch and talk about, the speech that they use, or the way they consume entertainment all either help or hinder their responsibility to be "dignified" is, for some, not even entertainable as a serious suggestion.

---

[2] See Carl Trueman, *The Rise and Triumph of the Modern Self: Cultural Amnesia, Expressive Individualism, and the Road to the Sexual Revolution* (Wheaton, IL: Crossway, 2020).

I can't think of anywhere where this juxtaposition of our cultural climate and Scripture's portrayal of a "dignified life" is more apparent than on social media. While it isn't the central reason I left social media a couple years ago,[3] the indignity so common on the platform is palpable now upon my (reluctant) return. I have not been back long, but in my short time back from the wilderness of my social media-less monastery, I have been battling culture shock. The shameless self-promotion; the self-congratulatory, self-righteous, self-asserting snobbery is intense. And before offering a hearty, internal "amen," let me just say—if I can play the part of a non-native with a tiny bit of external distance—these sorts of shenanigans are ubiquitous across the board. I have seen *pastors* and *scholars* behaving in the most disgraceful way on the internet. One person gets on and shamelessly promotes himself in the tackiest of ways, another person gets on and "subtweets" in the most sanctimonious of ways. One person skips good-faith interaction with an argument and instead goes straight to the ad hominem, another person comes from the other direction and does exactly the same. The sarcasm, the belligerence, the priggishness is, if I can speak frankly, *downright embarrassing.* It is like watching a friend at a party begin to lose his self-awareness. He laughs loudly, he tells an inappropriate story, he makes a joke that crosses the line—and you stand there thinking, *Please, Joe, stop! Keep your shirt on, stop talking, you're embarrassing yourself, and it's hard to watch!* I think most of us have built and unhealthy tolerance for this kind of unseemly, undignified behavior. We are desensitized, but that is no excuse.

Let me appear to change the topic for a moment. I promise I'm not. Let me tell you about an anecdote in the delightful little book by J.V. Fesko called *The Need for Creeds Today: Confessional Faith*

---

[3] See chapter 7.

in a Faithless Age.[4] In this book, Fesko shares the story of a "duel that almost was," during the Synod of Dort (1618–1619). At this Synod, delegates of various Dutch Reformed churches came together in response to the Five Articles of Remonstrance (1610), which were a handful of Arminian doctrinal objections to the Belgic Confession of Faith. The synod eventuated in the Canons of Dort—a marvelous example of theological precision—but not until after some death threats. Except, the death threats weren't between the Reformed pastors and their Arminian counterparts, but were advanced within the Synod itself! The culprit was Franciscus Gomarus, who challenged Matthias Maltinius to a duel after taking offense during a public debate at the synod.

The duel, obviously, never happened. But what Fesko points out is that no one considered the almost-duel as anything particularly unusual. There are a lot of reasons for this, but the point I'm making is that duels were socially acceptable and completely within cultural bounds. Does that mean that we are thereby required to cut Gomarus some slack? Well, that depends on what we mean by "slack." On the one hand, the kind of chronological snobbery that anachronistically places contemporary social expectations on figures of the past is not thoughtful or charitable, and those who engage in such snobbery should bear in mind the words of our Lord: "with the judgment you pronounce you will be judged, and with the measure you use it will be measured to you" (Matt 7:2). We should humbly show figures of the past the same respect we hope and pray our children and grandchildren and great-grandchildren will show us in the future. On the other hand, this kind of humility does not acquit Gomarus of all moral culpability for his actions. We are not moral subjectivists; if it is objectively immoral to normalize battles to the death over petty personal affronts in any age, it is objectively immoral in every age.

---

[4] J.V. Fesko, *The Need for Creeds Today: Confessional Faith in a Faithless Age* (Grand Rapids, MI: Baker Academic, 2020).

And as Fesko pointed out, John Davenant—a delegate who was *there* at the synod—objected to duels in the strongest possible terms, and he argued his case from his pulpit forcefully. That Davenant was a relatively lonely voice in this respect means that Gomarus's actions were both understandable and inexcusable.

I trust you get the connection I'm aiming for: what generally constitutes as socially acceptable does not determine what is truly dignified, in the Pauline sense of the word. If we aren't careful, our barometer for identifying shameful behavior can start to be calibrated by worldly standards, and we won't even know it. We can be pressed into the world's mold and totally miss the fact that what we consider outrageous and what we consider normal is not calibrated according to Scripture, but rather to a godless culture. Let us have the humility to acknowledge that, and endeavor to be John Davenants of the internet. Fesko makes this connection explicit: "All too often the vitriolic rhetoric of politics seeps into the church. The same is true of discourse on the internet. Theological debates on social media unfortunately read all too much like the heated exchanges that transpired between Gomarus and Martinius. Tempers flare, hearts seeth, and fingers type harsh words that fly through cyberspace and inflict damage on the souls of fellow Christians."[5]

It is not uncommon for me to float articles I write by some trusted voices—namely, my fellow elders—before publishing them. There are a couple of pieces that I wrote over the course of 2020 that never saw the light of day because some of my brother-pastors discouraged me from hitting "publish." At the time, while I was still in my social media-less monastery, I remember feeling hamstrung—like I couldn't share something I really enjoyed writing just because they had "thinner skin than me." I distinctly recall one conversation, wherein a brother-pastor told me a piece was

---

[5] Fesko, *The Need for Creeds Today*, 110.

too sarcastic. I told him that the sarcasm had to be received in the spirit in which it was given. "Imagine I said that line with a cheerful laugh and a smile on my face," I said, trying to convince him of the piece's innocuous nature, "it's not derision, it's Chestertonian cheekiness." His response was simple: "You've been off social media too long, Sam. People don't have ears for Chestertonian cheekiness there; it's so saturated with vitriol that people *will* read your article and miss anything but the sarcasm, and they will interpret it as nothing more than you being a jerk." Now, while I don't think I'll *ever* be able to purge my writing entirely of a little good-spirited Chestertonian cheekiness, I totally get his point now. It is downright tragic that the kind of relationship G.K. Chesterton had with H.G. Wells is virtually unconscionable in today's climate (i.e., a relationship in which they wrote public biting criticisms against one another while maintaining a meaningful friendship, without the slightest sense of contradiction), but it is what it is.

All that to say, I think there is a major shortage of "dignified living" on Christian Twitter. This is not a scolding, and if it reads that way, forgive me. I'm not angry, just embarrassed. Christ won't judge our words on a curve, as if a careless word spoken is more acceptable because it was spoken on Twitter where *everyone* speaks carelessly. The expectation to be dignified doesn't go away just because we happen to be living in a profoundly undignified culture. So, let's do better, shall we?

Chapter 10
Learning Gratitude (from Sir Roger Scruton)

They created a monster. In May, 1968, Roger Scruton (1944–2020) was a twenty-four-year-old student in Paris while the hopes and dreams of progressive revolutionaries unfolded in the form of riots. The old system had to go, so that—up from the ashes—a socialist utopia could arise. But ashes, after all, are made in only one way, so in May of 1968, Roger Scruton looked down from his balcony and watched as his peers set the streets of Paris ablaze. Many a zealous student saw the same sight, and the effect was (and *is*) all too common—a moth-like romance for fire burns in the bosom, and in they go, piously chanting whatever slogan happens to ring out at the time. For Scruton, however, the riots in Paris had the reverse effect. Instead of being the devouring fire of self-destruction and judgment they were for so many, they became for him the refining fire of consecration. A veil was lifted, and Scruton saw not a burgeoning and promising future in the revolutionary mindset, he saw a petulant adolescence, a child-like tantrum on the scale of genuine social upheaval. The instigators of these riots thought they were burning down all things conservative, but they were rather forging steel-spine conservativism at its best. Roger Scruton found his purpose.

I first became aware of Scruton when I determined that *beauty* would be central to my doctoral research, which made Scruton—one of the most formidable and important public intellectuals of the latter 20th and early 21st centuries—unavoidable. Having discovered the witty, soft-spoken philosopher, a lifelong engagement was inevitable. How could I not keep reading and listening to this prototypical figure? His house was littered with books, he wrote on beauty and architecture and conservatism and environmentalism and politics and short stories, he was classically trained on the piano, he lived his golden years living on a small farm, and he sported the most epic, perpetual bed-head (the kind that screams, "I'm an intellectual"); the attraction was predestined.

One of the reasons Scruton refreshes is that he did not play intellectual games. The meditation on beauty (which is really the central thread that ties *all* of his interests together) was not simply a vocational feature, nor a hobby; it was what Scruton survived on. He sought beauty like a starving man seeks bread, because that's what it is—it is bread for starving souls. This analogy of "food" is fitting in many ways. The pursuit of true beauty is the pursuit of *good* soul food. It's possible for someone to get by without going hungry, and yet never truly feed himself in a way that helps him flourish. A man who lives off of fast-food may not be starving, but he is impoverished nonetheless. He has not been properly *fed* in the full sense of the word. His diet is not a diet that satisfies, but rather one that merely gratifies.

And this is the thing Scruton lamented in terms of beauty and the modern world. He groaned when he saw western culture around him plunging headlong into "uglification." Of course, such categories require objective standards for "beauty" and "ugliness," which is anathema for many a philosopher today, but this was all further evidence for how ugly culture has become. A world incapable of distinguishing between the beautiful and the ugly is already a world deeply impoverished. What Scruton commended was a higher way. He highlights the contrast between "satisfaction" and "gratification"—between "kitsch" and "art;" between "surviving" and "living;" between "pornography" and "sexual intimacy;" between square buildings of cold glass and metal and florescent lights and cubicles on the one hand, and *home* on the other.

The pursuit of beauty is the path to satisfaction. It is hard, and requires work and sacrifice and cultivation—it involves your whole person in the pursuit of virtue. It is a path that requires attention and focus, and therefore is not easy, but it is reward-ing—it is the path that leads to the full embracing of one's human-ity, which means it brings with it *freedom*. The pursuit of the kitsch is the path of quick gratification. It's a short path and easy to travel on. You push a button, you get a jolt of sensation, an in-stant of gratification, and you move on. The problem with this short path is that it leads nowhere but where you began. You push the button again, and again, and again, and again, and before long the gratification wears off more quickly, your faculties have be-come numb, and you are a slave. This is the way of mere function. Fast-food, internet pornography, endless social media feeds, end-less hours of streaming (that are even advertised as "binge-wor-thy"), Lady Gaga mindlessly and monotonously hammering away on the same soul-suffocating note without a hint of melody and calling it a "song"—these are all the products of the way of "kitsch."

Another strength of Scruton is his celebration of *quiddity*. What Scruton commends (and demonstrates) is the discipline of pressing into the *quiddity* of this world. To absorb the "thisness" of everything. To take note of, and appreciate, the soft texture of *this* sofa, contrasted with the coolness of *this* hardwood floor on *my* bare feet, complimented by the soft warm light of *that* lamp and the crisp scrape of paper against *my* thumb, etc. Good poets throughout the century have trafficked in *quiddity*, and they serve us by inviting us to slow down and take note with gratitude. This is the very opposite of the sensation one gets while slumped over a smartphone, repeatedly swiping the glossy screen while images whiz by.

What we are describing is a choice between two different ways of being in the world. One way is to *take* and *use* and *exploit* in the spirit of self-entitled gratification. The other way is to *receive* and *enjoy* and *share* in a spirit of gratitude. People who live this way are markedly different. I think of figures like G.K. Chesterton or

C.S. Lewis—men who seem to be more alive than others. They were *awake* to the world around them, and they were grateful to exist.

And this way of being in the world—the way of gratitude—has a straight line to conservatism. And when I say "conservatism," I do not mean one particular "conservative" political party (like the United States National Republican Party, which is "conservative" only when graded on a curve against the Democratic Party, and that is not saying much), but rather *principled* conservatism. It is a spirit of gratitude, over and against a spirit of resentful revolution.

So, for example, classical conservative literary criticism invites the reader to step into the world of a book. It asks the reader to identify characters that embody virtue and then copy them. A conservative literary critic walks away from a work of literature having *learned something*—she is grateful for the lessons of the past.

A progressive literary critic, on the other hand, invites the reader to see *through* the work. Rather than stepping into the work as a student, the reader is to stand above the work as a judge— with the monochromatic lens of "power struggle." The progressive literary critic looks past the story itself to identify where the oppression is, where the exploitation is, and how the story itself functions in this same lens. The progressive literary critic walks away from a work of literature having explained nothing. She has explained it away—she is resentful of the past.

This revolutionary spirit breeds a cynicism that parasitically kills the culture it inherits. The progressive spirit is incapable of actually building anything, it is only capable of tearing down. In this way, the revolutionary spirit is cannibalistic—it devours the institutions and art and history and culture that gave it a voice to begin with. The end result is a baron wasteland. Right now, western universities give the impression of vitality, but this is only because their inheritance of Western Civilization has been so great. They who are in the business of *deconstructing* may feel as if things are bound to go on swimmingly like this for long, but it only feels that way because of how much *constructing* their forbearers engaged in. But the well will run dry. They will conclude their seemingly endless witch hunt to discover that there is no more culture left to criticize, because they've burnt it all down.

This is why Scruton's love for beauty is one and the same with his conservatism. Principled conservatism is simply the social and political manifestation of *gratitude*. It is the posture that looks to the past to receive the good, the true, and the beautiful, and then seeks to keep it safe and conserve it for the future.

This does not mean that a conservative is incapable of criticizing the past, or even changing institutions for the better. But prerequisite the willingness to *improve* is the acknowledgment of value. One must see the worth in the institutions or culture one is seeking to improve before it can be improved upon. There is something challenging and beautiful and praiseworthy about this kind of principled conservatism. The upshot of this way of thinking is that it infuses the adherent into the culture he gratefully inherits and then seeks to pass on down to others—he becomes part of it, with himself as a benefit to those around him. And this is because the grateful person is incandescent—he's taken in all the light and heat around him, and he radiates. The progressive, revolutionary personality, by contrast, is like a black hole. He devours. He is not grateful but is rather resentful and bitter. He is cynical.

Sir Roger Scruton was the photo negative of this kind of revolutionary personality. He would often joke around about how the Left is more naturally inclined to generate slogans that crowds could chant (i.e., "forward!" "change!" "down with ___!"). Scruton points out the conservatism is inhospitable to mob rationale— its slogan would be something like, "Hesitate!" which doesn't seem to roll off the tongue so easily in a chant. But it is an antidote for the illness Douglas Murray calls "the madness of crowds."

Scruton himself wrote polemically against such madness with not a little force. In *Fools, Frauds and Firebrands: The New Thinkers on the Left*, for example, Scruton launches a full-scale attack on such ideologies. In the end, Scruton ties up the entire leftist ideology, in all its various forms, with a neat bow, and then burns it to crisps. "The final result of the culture wars has been an enforced political correctness, by which the blasted landscape of art, history and literature is policed for the residual signs of racist, sexist, imperialist or colonialist way of thinking."[1] This is unavoidable, for (as Scruton points out) when Adorno offers us the absolute alternative between the capitalist system and utopia, he is being honest—and this honesty amounts to the absolute alternative between freedom and slavery.

Scruton is not silent about the genuine concerns raised by thinkers of the new left, even if he has no confidence in their diagnosis or prescription. It is true that capitalism is hospitable to a kind of vanity and materialistic decadence that commoditizes humans. In many ways, this is the definition of a twenty-first-century problem. For the leftist, this is proof that capitalism is Western society's original sin, and confession and repentance is therefore expressed as a culture of repudiation, which is committed to denouncing all things Western, and praising every culture but Western culture.

The problem is that justification, for the leftists, is by faith alone in the non-reality of utopian wish-thinking. It does not matter how many times the ideology is allowed to run its course—leaving body counts of millions in its wake—its utopian ideal provides an escape hatch for its proponents. "That was not *real*

---

[1] Roger Scruton, *Fools, Frauds and Firebrands: Thinkers of the New Left* (New York, NY: Bloomsbury, 2015), 275.

Marxism" is like a magic serum to raise dead philosophies that have no business getting up out of the grave.

Christians should take note and be warned. Appropriating language and categories of the left, while promising as a socially beneficial strategy in the short term, is a very bad strategy in the long run. We would be wise to heed Scruton's advice, and answer the unhealthy residual effects of sin working through a capitalistic society not with a society of slavery, but rather by strengthening those institutions and traditions that operate through free-association. Schools, clubs, and most centrally for the faithful Christian, local churches. This means hierarchy, of course, and we can say so cheerfully. But a defense of God's marvelous decision to make the cosmos hierarchical is for another essay.

We should not let Sir Roger Scruton fool us with his gentle tone, his philosopher's tussled hair, his irenic smile. What stood before us until January, 2020 as a beauty-loving, horse-riding, music-composing, wine-drinking gentlemen was actually an intellectual juggernaut. Time and again he lends the full force of his wit for our benefit. While many are dazzled by the illusory smoke-screening jargon of "anti-capitalism," "anti-hegemony," post-modern, utopian tomfoolery, Scruton walks into the room like a Marshwiggle with a burnt foot and declares in no uncertain terms (to mix references): "the emperor is in his birthday suit."

The current of western culture today pulls towards a way of being in the world that is marked by suspicion and cynicism—a way of conceptualizing all of human history in a neo-Marxist framework of power struggles between the haves and the have-nots. According to this way of thinking, the have-nots are virtuous by definition, and the haves are morally suspect by definition. With this reductionistic framework, morality is relativized: if you find yourself at the top of the power structure, your privilege prevents you from being virtuous, and if you find yourself at the bottom, anything goes—whatever you can do to climb up from underneath your oppression is morally justifiable. This way of thinking inspires a race to the bottom ("how shall I count the intersections I inhabit as a victim?") that actually *disincentivizes* a spirit of gratitude ("If I am grateful, that means I'm not oppressed, which means I'm the oppressor").

In contrast to this colorless and cold way of viewing the world, Scruton shows us a better way. Chesterton found it as well. He called it the "mystical minimum of gratitude." One author described Chesterton as "filled with both an enormous sense of thankfulness, and an enormous need for someone or something to thank."[2] This way of living—a way that would far rather be dumbfounded by the gratuity of life than resentful at what life isn't—is the way of living Roger Scruton advocated for. And this better way finds a natural home in the Christian life: "*I know how to be brought low, and I know how to abound. In any and every circumstance, I have learned the secret of facing plenty and hunger, abundance and need*" (Phil. 4:12).

---

[2] Frederick Buechner, *Speak What We Feel: Not What We Ought to Say* (New York, NY: HarperOne, 2006), 119.

Chapter 11
A New Kind of Racism
(A Review of *White Fragility*)

> *"Political speech and writing are largely the defense of the indefensible ... Political language—and with variations this is true of all political parties, from Conservatives to Anarchists—is designed to make lies sound truthful and murder respectable, and to give an appearance of solidity to pure wind."* George Orwell

Long gone are the days of my aspiration to be a professional culture-analyst. There was a time when I grew excited at the prospect of being the one to respond to hot button topics with hot takes in a hot tone. Slow and steady was the realization that this is owing not to a sacred destiny to be "the cultural engagement guy," but more to a primal temperament to never shy away from a fight. Such a temperament is by no means intrinsically virtuous (though I am told it can be applied virtuously when directed toward noble ends, and indeed, I have seen it happen in the case of stronger men). This realization occasioned the slow death of the ambition to be a professional culture-analyst. That dream took a turn for the worst when I became a pastor (that glorious, heart-softening vocation) and its final croak was when all social media accounts bearing my name went the way of Enoch ("Enoch walked with God, and he was not" [Gen. 5:24]).

All that to say, I tread this precarious ground not as an aspiring culture-analyst, but as a Christian and a pastor. I have seen this book recommended by many a Christian, and thought it therefore merited critical engagement. *What ought Christians think about*

Robin DiAngelo's book, White Fragility?[1] That is the question I wish to answer with this chapter.

There are a lot of great insights in this book, and we should praise them. There are things white Americans need to hear that DiAngelo says. Many middle-class, white Americans assume a certain level of normativity with their experience within this country, and diversifying perception can be a powerful thing. More than once, while reading *White Fragility*, I was left with egg on my face at the recollection of painful or offensive interactions I have had with black friends. This is not a bad thing, and Christians—those who have a vested interest in loving *truth*—should be discontent at the prospect of blissful ignorance. We should want the truth. And the truth is that living as a black person in America is simply going to be different than living as a white person in America.

Some of the experiential divergence is owing to the fact that the majority of Americans are white and a fraction are black, but *many* of the visceral differences of experience are owing to the radically racialized nature of our country—a feature not destined by circumstance, but created by a history of racism. It's messy, and no amount of "color blindness" is going to unscramble that egg. Some of DiAngelo's observations on the historical development of racism and the process of racialization are therefore very good, and very helpful. So there's that.

But the valuable things in this book are crowded out by the high concentration of preposterous ideas that elbow their way to the front and leap off the page. And this is because the philosophical underpinnings for the whole project are disastrous from the beginning. There is poison in the well. But then again, this is perhaps not saying it quite strong enough. It is not simply that the well is poisoned, rather the majority is poison, with some water

---

[1] Robin DiAngelo, *White Fragility: Why It's So Hard for White People to Talk About Racism* (Beacon Press, 2018).

sprinkled in. It is a pernicious and thinly veiled repackaging of postmodernism—of Michel Foucault's variety, to be specific, which is the worst kind because it most often, as in the case for *White Fragility*, cozies up to Marxist sentiments.[2]

The fundamental mantra of this way of thinking is something like, "Power is everything." The entirety of human civilization, in this way of thinking, has been man-handled along by one oppressive system at a time. In this un-reality, the world is divided sharply between the oppressors (the privileged) and the oppressed (the victims). This relativizes virtue and vice arbitrarily. The privileged are, by virtue of their privilege, morally suspect–guilty until proven innocent. The oppressed, by virtue of their victimhood, are morally virtuous–righteous until proven otherwise.

Those who occupy places of privilege, whether they are conscious of this reality or not, are always and in every way motivated to maintain their power at the expense of the victimized. This means that the right way to analyze the privileged is not to take them at their word, but to read the privilege-grabbing motivation *behind* their word. Only this kind of suspicion could give rise to a statement like, "We must continue to ask how our racism manifests, not if."[3] Such a statement is as enlightening as it is brief. Not only does it bespeak an utter hopelessness with respect to the issue DiAngelo is inviting her readers to engage in (i.e., "Come and be rid of racism…which will never go away"), it also bodes well for the future of grievance studies: a population that is invited to ask

---

[2] Those who might consider this relationship innocuous may benefit from a reminder of Marxism's body count during the 20th century. Over 100 million. The bloodiest century of human history, and these numbers are irrespective of the also horrifying body count of fascism in the form of Nazism. For some reason, however, it is fashionable to decry fascism but proudly tout Marxist communism, even though the death toll of the latter exceeded the former.

[3] DiAngelo, *White Fragility*, 138.

always *how* their personal racism is manifest and never *if* it is will never be in want of demand for more books like *White Fragility*.

The paradigm of "power" as the interpretive grid for reality has many other strange consequences. One such consequence is the reductionistic assumption that inequality of outcome *must* and *can only* be explained by an abuse of power. "If we truly believe that all humans are equal," writes DiAngelo, "then disparity in condition can only be the result of systemic discrimination."[4] "Only" is, in this case, a very strong word. One might be more than willing to concede that many cases of disparity today—specifically, the differences between average white and black Americans—have systemic discrimination in its list of ingredients. Slavery, Jim Crow terrorism that birthed the Mass Migration, red-lining and the like have long-term effects. Ghettos are not created in a vacuum. But "*only*"?

What if the reasons for the disparity of outcomes are not *exclusively* external, systemic oppressive measures that created disadvantaged communities, but also includes the cultural shift in those communities (largely brought about by governmental intervention measures that were designed to help)? What if the disparity has more causes than racism, like fatherlessness? What if fatherlessness has more causes than mass incarceration, and what if mass incarceration has more causes than racism? What if the corruption of human civilization runs much deeper than a socially constructed commitment to the idea of "race?" What if there are more injustices than the injustice of racism? And further, what if not every occurrence of disparity of condition is indicative of an injustice at all?[5] This is a "what if" that will not do for DiAngelo, however, whose pre-commitments requires her to find "racism" at the bottom of every problem, real or imagined.

---

[4] DiAngelo, *White Fragility*, 17.
[5] See, Thomas Sowell, *Discrimination and Disparities* (Basic Books, New York: NY, 2018).

But just what is *racism*? This is an important point to work through, especially as Christians, who have a biblical mandate to concern themselves with racism. Christians recognize racism as a sin against God. And this is because man is made in the image of God (Gen. 1:26–28), and God's purpose from the beginning was always to have a kingdom of multi-ethnic, multi-lingual image bearers, who have multiplied and filled the earth with praise— praise ringing from a multitude of languages, from a multitude of lips, on the bodies shaded by a multitude of skin colors. This was always God's plan. He was working towards it when he promised Abraham that he and his descendants would be a blessing to the nations (Gen. 12). He was working towards it when he announced that Israel would be third "with Egypt and Assyria, a blessing in the midst of the earth" (Is. 19:24–25). He was working towards it when the eternal Son of God took on flesh as a Jew to be a Shepherd not only to a flock of Jews, but also Gentiles (Jn. 10:16). And he will complete this work in dazzling manner in the end (Rev. 7:9–10). For the Christian, racism—the dividing wall of hostility that separates ethnicities with animus tribal-superiority—is a sin against God. It is a blasphemous rejection of the gospel—the good news that Christ tears down such dividing walls with his equalizing work of atonement (Eph. 2:11–18).

While racism, like every other sin, can and does impact society on an institutional level, it is at root a prideful tendency to see one's tribe as superior to another's. Like every other sin, racism ought to be confessed and repented. Like every other *sin*, racism can only be forgiven by virtue of the blood of Jesus. Like every other sin, racism can be a shaping force within a culture or institution. Like every other *sin*, racism can only be progressively overcome by the work of the Spirit. And like every other *sin*, racism is objectively defined by God's revelation.

How does DiAngelo define racism? Not like this, of course. This fact in itself does not disqualify her from offering anything of value to our understanding of racism. Conceptually, it is possible for a true overlap of wisdom on account of God's common grace. So, her falling short of a robust, biblical definition of racism does not disqualify her from offering anything of value here, the thing that disqualifies her from such is her postmodern and subjective redefinition of racism. Racism, for DiAngelo, has no definite edges (which makes it hard for a Christian to co-sign her definition—we need definite edges if it is *sin* of which to be *repented*). For DiAngelo, racism is all about power, which means only the more socially dominant side on the dividing wall of hostility (however "dominance" is determined) can rightly be called "racist." "People of color may also hold prejudices and discriminate against white people, but they lack the social and institutional power that transforms their prejudice and discrimination into racism; the impact of their prejudice on whites is temporary and contextual."[6] And again, "When I say that only whites can be racist, I mean that in the United States, only whites have the collective social and institutional power and privilege over people of color. People of color do not have this power and privilege over white people."[7]

This road, we cannot walk down with DiAngelo. Sin is no respecter of ethnicity or social class or privileged station. If we are to retain the conception of racism as *sin* (and as Christians, we must), we cannot allow ourselves to buy into the reduction. It is to say that one man, by virtue of his skin color and no other reason, cannot commit one sin, while another man, by virtue of *his* skin color and no other reason, *cannot avoid* committing that sin. This is not how Scripture describes sin.

DiAngelo would have us redefine racism and "white superiority" so as to apply a-morally to *individuals* within *a broader social system*. Racism, for her, is not a personal sin, so much as it is a

---

[6] DiAngelo, *White Fragility*, 22.
[7] DiAngelo, *White Fragility*, 22.

system into which people are born. This is problematic for the above reasons regarding definition of sin and repentance, but it is also disingenuous at face level. She insists over and again that racism is not about "good people" and "bad people," but systems. Yet she seems to speak out of both sides of her mouth, because she then goes on to illustrate individual complicity within this larger social system in explicitly *moral terms*:

> For example, I have often heard whites dismissively say, "Just because of the color of my skin, I have privilege." Statements like this describe privilege as if it's a fluke— something that just happens to us as we move through life, with no involvement or complicity on our part. Critical race scholar Zeus Leonardo critiques the concept of white privilege as something white people receive unwittingly. He says that this concept is analogous to suggesting that a person could walk through life with other people stuffing money into his or her pockets without any awareness or consent on the walker's part. Leonardo challenges this conceptualization, which positions white privilege as innocence, by arguing that "for white racial hegemony to saturate everyday life, it has to be secured by a process of domination, or those acts, decisions, and policies that white subjects perpetrate on people of color."[8]

Thus, DiAngelo simultaneously claims that racism is not about being "good or bad" while also saying white privilege is *sustained* by "domination." "Domination" and "a-moral" do not go together. So, which is it? The reader is left wondering.

Another striking feature about the book is its dubious political nature. Being against racism, as it turns out, necessitates a monolithic political conviction. "Divesting of whiteness" looks like being sufficiently (i.e., radically) Left. The politically conservative,

---

[8] DiAngelo, *White Fragility*, 63–64.

white, non-racist is, for her, an oxymoron. One ought not fret with the obvious example of non-white political conservatives either; DiAngelo has a ready-made explanation for why they do not count in such discussions:

> Whites control all major institutions of society and set the policies and practices that others must live by. Although rare individual people of color may be inside the circles of power—Colin Powell, Clarence Thomas, Marco Rubio, Barack Obama—they support the status quo and do not challenge racism in any way significant enough to be threatening.[9]

(Of course, Obama is not a "non-white political *conservative*" in an objective sense, but yesterday's progressive liberal is today's right-wing extremist.)

All of these are reasons Christians should stop recommending *White Fragility*, but the strongest reason is the book's central contention. What makes *White Fragility* so sinisterly ingenious is its central non-falsifiable claim. DiAngelo has managed to make an argument that cannot be penetrated, because even the challenge of it is, in a strange twist, made to be its confirmation. How can a white man possibly challenge DiAngelo's book on *White Fragility* without his challenge being interpreted as a throbbing and pitiful display of his own *white fragility?* He cannot. His argument can always be dismissed as his white fragility vs. *White Fragility*.

This is a non-falsifiable claim, which means it is a non-starter for genuine critical engagement. If one can construct a system of thought that is so closed off that no argument can actually challenge it—a system that refuses to take any challenge at face value, but instead reads *through* the challenge, and explains it away as reinforcing the central claim—one has constructed a system of

---

[9] DiAngelo, *White Fragility*, 27.

thought that is fundamentally totalitarian. It cannot abide descent, so it is hedged and guarded and monitored on every conceivable side. If a white person moves out of a black neighborhood, that is white flight and racist; if a white person moves into a black neighborhood, that is gentrification and racist;[10] if a white person challenges any part of this book, that is just his white fragility flaring up; if a black person challenges any part of this book, that is because he has bought into whiteness and is experiencing Stockholm syndrome toward the oppressive structures around him.

In this book's world, the only non-racist is the white person who agrees entirely with its content, and the only authentically black person is the one who agrees entirely as well. It is internally brittle and needs to be protected with an outer shell that staves off reality itself. And this causes DiAngelo to say astounding things as if they were axiomatically self-evident, like, for example positing that "race, *like gender, is socially constructed.*"[11] Or that white women's tears are terrorist attacks on black people.[12] Or that *objectivity* is an *ideology* characteristic of oppressive white

---

[10] DiAngelo, *White Fragility*, 92.

[11] DiAngelo, *White Fragility*, 15. I agree, of course, that there is only the human race, and the decision to substitute "race" for "ethnicity" was a move on the part of Darwinian racists who sought to justify their claim that black people are biologically inferior to white. But to throw "gender" into that category, as if it somehow *clarifies* the point about social construction instead of obscuring it, is absurd.

[12] DiAngelo, *White Fragility*, 132. This is the theme of DiAngelo's chapter, "White Women's Tears": "White women's tears in cross-racial interactions are problematic for several reasons connected to how they impact others. For example, there is a long historical backdrop of black men being tortured and murdered because of a white woman's distress, and we white women bring these histories with us. Our tears trigger the terrorism of this history, particularly for African Americans." DiAngelo, *White Fragility*, 132. According to DiAngelo, the tears of white women are triggering and harmful for black men and women, except of course, when they are not: "I have certainly been moved to tears by someone's story in cross-racial discussions. And I imagine that sometimes tears are appreciated, as they can validate and bear witness to the pain of racism for people of color." DiAngelo, *White Fragility,* 136.

supremacy.[13] Such an outlandish claim is the ultimate barricade of self-protection, for how else can ideas be challenged if not on appeals to objective reality? If, by chance, one can turn *objectivity* into a feature of racism, one has secured total immunity to claim *anything*. Because, of course, who has to hear out an argument when it is grounded in objectivity if objectivity is *racist*?

It should be said at the close of this essay that white Christians have earned a bad reputation for understanding and engaging in the unique struggles of their black neighbors (and their black brothers and sisters in Christ, for that matter).[14] This is tragic because Christianity is internally strapped with all the theological and philosophical resources necessary to lead the fray in both diagnosing the problem of racism, and prescribing its cure. The Critical Race Theory (CRT) DiAngelo propagates in *White Fragility* lacks the resources for both, and yet, CRT sociologists have done us a service in highlighting the *problem* of racialization in America.

This need not worry any Christians who, like myself, see no reconciliation between CRT and Christian theology. If someone points to the sky and says, "look, a bird!" but upon further inspection you conclude it is a plane, you need not say, "You were wrong

---

[13] DiAngelo, *White Fragility*, 9.

[14] Jamar Tisby has documented the long history of white Christian complicity in the horror of racism in *The Color of Compromise: The Truth about the American Church's Complicity in Racism* (Zondervan, Grand Rapids: MI, 2020). It should not be surprising at all that I offer this commendation with the caveat that much of its content is problematic (particularly his concluding chapter and its section on reparations). The first half of the book, that which works with objective standards for racism and white superiority, is pretty good. It is when he begins to cover the end of the twentieth, into the twenty-first century, that his narrative begins to fall off the rails. This is because as postmodernism began to take its toll in academia around this time, and new politicized definitions of racism begin to take shape, Tisby uncritically begins to work with those definitions. How he defines "racism" at the beginning of the book is radically distinct from how he defines it toward the end. Ultimately, Tisby reduces the act of white Christians voting Republican to an act of complicity with racism. This means that simply "voting Red" functions (at best) as one more non-loving act in the long history of Christian complicity with racism, which is far too simplistic, to say the least.

about the bird, there is *nothing* there." They saw *something*, even if it was misidentified. The same is true for many of the dominating CRT voices in recent years. They see *something*. But their system is impoverished of the resources both to diagnose the problem and to prescribe its cure. Therefore, the Christian ought to say to DiAngelo (and to CRT, more widely), "thank you," and "no thank you." "'Thank you' for pointing out this general area. But 'no thank you' to your framework for understanding it or your suggestions for what to do about it. I have seen where they go, and it is not pretty."

Christianity and CRT are water and oil. While they do not mix at the essential level, you can still ruin perfectly clean water by *trying* to mix it with oil. But no improvement comes of it. What it produces is nothing but cynicism, mistrust, and despair. It has the potential for strengthening nothing. I was once told by a white father of three Ethiopian children that a colleague of his, convinced by this wicked ideology, said something along the following lines to his black children, in his hearing: "You know, your daddy is a racist. And he will struggle with racism for the rest of life." Now, if you are committed to sowing suspicion and bitterness in young hearts for the purpose of eroding strong family ties, I cannot think of a more effective thing to say. But if the intent is for fathers and their (adopted) children to tie bonds of trust, where fathers do not provoke their children to anger and children obey their fathers in godly submission, there is no friendship to be had with CRT. The blended family is not safe. The interracial marriage is not safe. The prerequisite of trust and security is undermined from the start with CRT.

Chapter 12
Pride (or, On Theological Jerks)

It is possible to make a sound point in a conversation as a jerk. It is possible to have sound theology as a jerk. It's possible to be a high-scoring seminarian-jerk. As I have meditated on this tragic phenomenon, I have reached the conclusion that one of the most overlooked spiritual disciplines—especially for seminarians and those who are more theologically-minded—is the conscious effort to not be a jerk. "Pursue humility" is another way of saying it, but I think "don't be a jerk" cuts to the heart in a way jerks need (speaking from experience).

Let me illustrate my point with an example from the world of comedy. Now, stand-up comedy is becoming an increasingly difficult entertainment space to enter as a Christian. My wife and I are elated when we see "TV-14" or "TV-PG" next to a comedy special on Netflix. But there are still comedians out there whom one can consistently depend upon to make you laugh with an intact conscience. Jim Gaffigan does that for me. Once a comedian has gained your trust as a consistently funny performer, your expectations correspond with that trust. So, when you see him stroll across the platform, you gear up in preparation to laugh. You expect to be tickled.

This happens in all relationships, not merely in distant ones like those between professional comedians and their fans. Your habitual behavior towards others produces expectations. For better or worse, others develop impressions of you that are largely, though not always, informed by your consistent patterns of verbal and non-verbal communication. My expectation when I see Jim Gaffigan is to laugh. And I think it is important, from time to time, to ask ourselves what people expect from us, and how those expectations are informed by our consistent behaviors.

What do I elicit from others? Flinching? Dread? The expectation to be belittled or cut down or insulted or railed at or lectured?

Now, there is a danger if this exercise is taken too far. Ear-tickling, people-pleasing, man-fearing, truth-compromising, and all that. But I think it is entirely possible (necessary for faithfulness, in fact) to be absolutely unwavering on convictional truth matters and still give people the expectation to receive love and compassion from you.

Ray Ortlund is a great example. What Jim Gaffigan does for my expectation to laugh, Ray Ortlund does for my expectation to be encouraged. And anyone who knows the preaching ministry of Ray will know that the accusation of ear-tickling will not stick—he is a faithful preacher, which means he preaches hard, convicting, sin-naming, rebuking words because those are the Bible's words. But you never have to guess whether or not he preaches those difficult words as a lover of his audience. He loves people. He has compassion for people, even while offending them with the gospel. I want to be like that.

Now, our convictions, in and of themselves, often do offend others. That is okay. Occasionally, it is even good. If your opinions are not offensive to *someone*, it's because you are either dishonest or a spineless, opinionless jellyfish, neither of which are commendable. This notwithstanding, we should not just assume that if people dread interacting with us it is because the truth in our words sting. That might be the case. Or maybe people dread interacting with us because we are jerks. Faithfulness isn't merely a matter of what we believe and communicate, but also *how* we communicate what we believe.

This is a perennial concern for me because I routinely find myself sympathizing with positions that are often associated with jerks. Allow me to catalogue for you my greatest hits of controversial positions.

- I am a Calvinist. And not just the under-the-breath, kind-of-embarrassed-to-say-it-out-loud kind of Calvinist. I'm a black-coffee Calvinist who happens to think that "L" is one of the tulip's loveliest peddles.
- I'm a complementarian, and not the "thin" version, either. I affirm the hierarchal nature of the cosmos, and I think the complementary distinctions between men and women are not arbitrarily applied to the local church and the home, but run all the way down. They are a part of the natural order and have implications all throughout society.
- I still believe in penal substitutionary atonement. The scarlet stained cross is infinitely lovely in my estimation, and "wrath" and "punishment" and "judgment" and "propitiation" are all concepts that don't embarrass me in the slightest.
- I am persuaded by the arguments of family integrated worship on Sunday mornings.
- As if I wasn't already "asking for it," I am fully persuaded by the case for classical Christian education, or something very much like it. In fact, the older I get, and the more our culture plunges into paganism, the more unwise I consider the voluntary decision of Christian parents to send their children to public school.

Now, if you found yourself hooting and hollering as you read any of the above, read these words carefully: *do not be a jerk*. The camps represented by the topics I just described are stereotypically characterized as jerks for a reason. We are the ones who often fail to care for the human beings we talk to more than we care about proving them wrong. It should bother us that the fruit of our pet-theologies are consistently hard, unkind, abrasive people who demonstrate zero compassion for those who disagree.

We should hold our position with grace and humility, and never let it become more precious to us than the person you are talking to about it. And we should maintain proportion, because, believe it or not, you can worship alongside a person who disagrees with you about the doctrines of grace, or education without compromising. Furthermore, you can communicate your position to that same person without belittling or bullying them. On the flipside, it is possible to hold the correct position in an argument and yet be the one in the wrong simply by communicating the right thing as a jerk.

Of course, it never feels this way, especially for those awakening to new ideas. Where new discoveries of theological topics abound, the process of developing conviction is intoxicating. When we go down a rabbit hole that opens us up to a whole new exciting conversation, we throw ourselves into the study. That is good. Studying should be exciting, and it is right for research topics to enjoy a large portion of our thoughts for a time. The problem is, after having thought little of anything besides the topic in question for months, our conviction on that topic begins to overshadow everything else. We feel justified in beating every person over the head with our position because "It's the truth, and truth matters!" Every hill begins to look like a good spot to die. In other words, we begin thinking that if we are correct jerks, our correctness will outweigh our jerkiness. Our conviction begins to resemble a hammer, and people begin to resemble nails. But people are not nails.

If we are not careful, church unity will be sacrificed for pet-theologies, and the bar for what constitutes as a church-splitting-worthy issue will take a nose dive into a valley that only other seminarians know even exists. That is worse than being wrong about (insert your theological hobby horse.) Calvinists are not the only ones who need cages for a time.

Chapter 13
On Brokenness

A small group of members from a local church gather on couches and chairs in a member's home to discuss the previous Sunday's sermon. They share insights, encourage each other, laugh, and gravely confess sin. So far, so good. Then, one member begins to revel in the grace of God and his utter dependence thereof, saying something along the lines of, "I'm just so needy. I always need grace. And what a relief it is to know God wants me like this! He wants me needy and eager for his grace so I can rejoice in my weakness. My neediness and finitude and brokenness is a good thing!" What's wrong with this picture? Well, it really depends on what he means by "brokenness" and what he means by "a good thing."

Recently, Jared Wilson wrote a timely article on why we should hang on to the language of "brokenness."[1] In that article, he stressed the importance of distinguishing between "brokenness" and "sin." His point is that if we flatten those two concepts, we often burden victims, who already feel a misplaced guilt for the brokenness they are experiencing, with *more* guilt. Sometimes people are broken and have nothing to repent of with respect to that brokenness. Victims really do exist, and often they feel guilty for no good reason. As Jared says, "We further traumatize victims when we tell them their wounds are sins." This is an important point to make, and as a pastor who routinely sees this kind of misplaced guilty conscience among the members of my church, I'm thankful to Jared for making it.

---

[1] Jared C. Wilson, "Why We Should Use the Language of Brokenness," *The Gospel Coalition* (Published on February 21, 2018. https://www.thegospelcoalition.org/blogs/jared-c-wilson/use-language-brokenness/. Accessed on November 3, 2020).

I would like to make an additional point. There is a difference between affirming and applauding broken people as they come to Jesus, and affirming and applauding the brokenness itself. That difference is difficult to mark out in practice, but it is important that we labor to do just that. It is the difference between praising God for overcoming an obstacle and praising the obstacle itself. It is the difference between praising a craftsman for making beautiful work with shoddy materials, and insisting that shoddy materials are superior to sound ones.

Although brokenness is distinguishable from sin, they are nevertheless connected. There is no such thing as brokenness that has no relation whatsoever to sin. It is what sin leaves behind after reeking its carnage. Sometimes brokenness is caused by one's own sin, sometimes it's caused by another's sin, and sometimes it's caused by God in order to sanctify such a person—and he does this by using the effects of the fall, which came about through sin (Is. 45:7; 48:8–10; 2 Cor. 12:7–10). That last point should be stated and restated explicitly.

Sometimes God breaks people by ordaining for this fallen world to sanctify—to "holi-fy"—them. God breaks them to purge them of sin, or to protect them from sin, or to help give them a distaste for sin, or even to simply fit them for a sinless heaven. But, no matter the scenario, sin and brokenness are never totally unrelated. There would be no brokenness if it weren't for the fall, and we long to see the complete reversal of the fall and its effects. This means we eagerly wait for the binding up of all broken things—both brokenness which is caused by our personal sin and that which isn't. We don't *like* brokenness. In fact, we very much would like to bid it farewell.

This is where nuance is important (and tricky) though, because what we *do* like is our *finitude*. That's something to celebrate! Our dependency is not a bug or a defect in itself; fundamentally, we are needy, contingent beings, and our finitude is a design feature that glorifies God and works for our joy. This was true of mankind before Adam and Eve disobeyed God, and it will be true of mankind after Christ returns to judge the living and the dead.

The problem is, at present, our *awareness* of our finitude is typically occasioned by *brokenness*. We are always experiencing neediness, but we're generally asleep to it. But brokenness makes us keenly *aware* of our neediness. In this way, God uses brokenness to our advantage. This is why Paul can be thankful for his thorn in the flesh, and you can be thankful for:

- The cancer in your blood, i.e. brokenness that comes from living in a broken world.
- The shambled state you're left in after looking at porn, i.e. brokenness that comes from sinning.
- The fragility you're left in after being abused, i.e. brokenness that comes from being sinned against.[2]

It is possible, as impossible as it sounds, to praise God for these forms of brokenness because they refine us in ways of which we are seldom aware. Paul doesn't say: "This light momentary affliction might be preparing for us an eternal weight of glory beyond all comparison. Who knows?" There is no maybe. Affliction prepares us for glory. Bank on it (2 Cor. 4:17–18).

God sanctifies his people through suffering—and, in a sense, he is no respecter of where that suffering comes from. Think

---

[2] This, obviously, is an explosive statement, and I don't intend to make it with a cavalier attitude. The promises of God working "*all things* together for good for those who love him" (Rom. 8:28), and using (what never feels like) "light and momentary affliction" to prepare "an eternal weight of glory" (2 Cor. 4:17–18) are promises that should be uttered with grave, sensitive, compassionate sobriety when abuse is in view. But those promises are *there*. And they are sweet for those who have eyes to see and ears to hear that God is both *sovereign* and *good*, and that he uses every form of suffering for sanctification, including the suffering inflicted by another. And this in no way minimizes the seriousness of the sin committed by the abuser, rather, it magnifies the grace and goodness of God to use that sin for the benefit of the abused.

about it: is God prepared to reject any form of suffering as unusable for the sanctification of his people? Whether it's from your sin, the sins of others, or from God sovereignly ordaining and using impersonal effects of the fall: if you are experiencing suffering, God is at work to sanctify. And, as God sanctifies with the instrument of suffering through brokenness, he is revealing to us the finitude we will experience long after our brokenness is mended. The things brokenness reveals (neediness and finitude) are good, and to the degree that brokenness reveals it, we can be thankful for such an instrument. But this does not mean we should celebrate the instrument itself. Our gratitude isn't intrinsically in brokenness, our gratitude is in God for what he does with brokenness.

This is difficult for us to wrap our minds around because the world we live in basically has two speeds: shame or pride, embarrassment or affirmation. But Jesus is not so reductionistic as that. He invites all the weary people to come to him, shamelessly, but his invitation to all the weary people is not to come and have their weariness affirmed. It's to come and receive rest so as to not feel weary anymore (Matt. 11:28–30). His invitation to the broken is to come to him in order to be fixed! Of course, on this side of eternity, no one will be completely and finally fixed of their brokenness, but make no mistake, he has begun that work, and he will finish it. Faithful Christianity is content with nothing less than absolute restoration. We don't want a hint of brokenness in heaven. We don't want a smidgen of brokenness to be left alone or "affirmed."

We can, and should, tell people to feel absolutely no shame in confessing that they struggle with depression, or doubt, or self-loathing, or persistent wounds from those who have wronged them. They shouldn't feel embarrassed to reveal their pride, or insecurities, or lust, or same-sex attraction, or envy. Those things describe broken people—regardless of whether their brokenness was caused by personal sin or not. And the good news for them is that Jesus came to redeem broken people, and broken people only. The gospel is only for those kinds of people. There are no demands to figure out how to not be broken anymore before coming to Jesus. He doesn't want whole people (none exist, by the way), he only wants broken people. But the great news of the gospel is that broken people don't have to stay broken forever. Jesus loves fixer-uppers because he loves to fix them up.

If we come to him, and bashfully introduce ourselves, we will not be shamed for our lack of sophistication. We won't be snickered at for limping, or crawling. We won't be scoffed at for our shabby attire. He won't ever recoil in disgust from our disfigurements, whatever they may be. But he also won't leave us exactly how we came. That would not at all be loving. No, he'll do something much better! He'll embrace us and fix our brokenness. He'll set those bones in place so we can walk without a limp. He'll give us his ever new, clean robes of righteousness. And he will mend our disfigurements.

Although this work won't finally be completed until the consummation of his Kingdom on Earth, he has nevertheless begun the work now. Jesus invites us broken to come, shamelessly, with no embarrassment for our destitution. And when we do, he doesn't show his love for us by looking at our brokenness and saying, "That looks cute, you should keep that." No, he shows his love for us by saying, "Don't you worry about that, I'm going to fix it. Let me put a little grace here. Give you some Holy Spirit-wrought power there. A touch of local church discipleship, brothers and sisters to weep with you while you weep and rejoice with you while you rejoice, a lifetime of sanctifying suffering, a resurrection… and…voilà! I am making all things new!" He shows his love for us not by affirming our brokenness, but by receiving us while still in such a state, and then slapping an expiration date on it.

Chapter 14
Against Cancel Culture

In the middle of the twentieth century, two novels were produced by two geniuses on, generally, similar topics. In 1948, George Orwell's book, *1984*, was published, and four years earlier, C.S. Lewis published *That Hideous Strength*. Both imagine a similar dystopian world, overrun by totalitarians—"Big Brother" and the "the Party" are the antagonists in *1984*, and in *That Hideous Strength*, it is the National Institute of Co-ordinated Experiments (N.I.C.E.). Both novels utilize the notion of newspeak, double speak, the reduction of language for the purpose of domination, thought crimes, etc. Both novels imagine what *the abolition of man* might look like in a developed society. And both novels recognize the potency of technological advancements as a potential for great harm when allied with a utilitarian group-think mentality—a mentality that seeks to manipulate and control the masses for "efficiency's sake."

The differences, however, are stark. Orwell's classic imagines this dystopian future, strictly speaking, *under the sun*. Above Winston Smith's dreary and surveillance head was only sky; no heaven above, no hell below. Which means Big Brother was under no one, and therefore, *1984* ends in utter despair. The totalitarians made their way to the top and subsequently stayed there. O'Brian was absolutely right when he coldly assured Winston that "the rule of the Party is forever." The same cannot be said of the hellscape created by the N.I.C.E. in *That Hideous Strength*. This is, after all, the third and final installment of a sci-fi trilogy, and is the first and only volume set primarily on *earth*. Above Mark Studdock's head is no void; above his head are the Medieval heavens, brimming with life and potency. In fact," the N.I.C.E. essentially build themselves a Babel—they know there is a lot going on "out there, and they want to have a say in the matter. While Big Brother has no one to answer to, the N.I.C.E. reach up for deep heaven, and then pull down deep heaven on their heads. This is why *That Hideous Strength's* happy ending is unavoidable. The cosmos of *1984* is empty. The vacuum is filled with human power. The cosmos of Lewis's Ransom trilogy is inhabited from top to bottom, and is governed by God himself. Eventual reckoning for the N.I.C.E. is inevitable.

Both the commonalities and the differences of *1984* and *That Hideous Strength* teach us something about "cancel culture." This phenomenon, of course, is that ugly and putrid fruit that grows organically from the tree of post-modernism. "Theory," or "Critical Theory," after all, is little more than "cancel culture" at the core—it is a self-justifying witch hunt, which seeks to explain nothing, while explaining *away* everything. The "culture of repudiation"—as Roger Scruton calls it—is a culture of ascension by domination; standing tall by standing on other people's heads. To stay still and mind one's business, in this culture, is to get left behind and resign oneself to being stood on. Yesterday's progressive is today's bigot. Yesterday's feminist is today's sexist (just ask J.K. Rowling—whose comments about transgenderism and subsequent cancelation has eventuated in expensive tattoo removals or coverups for many jaded Harry Potter fans). If one desires to have one's credentials up to date, one must be vigilant for institutions and parties and people and practices to "call out." It is telling that power plays such a central role in cancel culture. It is not coincidental that those who myopically restrict their lives to *searching for power dynamics* end up being those who abuse others with illegitimate power grabs. Should it surprise us that those who are obsessed with power *act like they are obsessed with power*?

So, what might this sort of thing look like? Enumerating the victims of cancel culture is impossible, not because of a dearth of examples, but because of the ubiquity of examples. Consider this one. At the beginning of January 2020, if you were a New Yorker interested in such things, you may have been excited about a forthcoming event at the New York Public Library called "An Evening with Cancelled Women." It was supposed to be something of a roundtable discussion, featuring six feminists who could not keep up with the Leftward racing locomotive of progressivism—specifically, they made the mistake of hanging on to definitions of "feminism" that were two years too old—and were left eating dust. But if you were such a New Yorker at the beginning of January 2020, you would have been disappointed by the end of January 2020, for "An Evening with Canceled Women" was, of course, cancelled.[1]

Another (deliciously ironic) display of these shenanigans occurred (as is most often the case) on Twitter in the summer of 2020. *Harper's Magazine* published "A Letter on Justice and Open Debate."[2] The general thrust of the letter could be summarized as "cancel culture is bad." They write, "The free exchange of information and ideas, the lifeblood of a liberal society, is daily becoming more constricted." They express concern for the wide adoption of "an intolerance of opposing views, a vogue for public shaming and ostracism, and the tendency to dissolve complex policy issues in a blinding moral certainty." Lest they give the impression that this letter bespoke a drift into conservatism, the brave authors of the letter offered this irrelevant dig, "The forces of illiberalism are gaining strength throughout the world and have a powerful ally in Donald Trump, who represents a real threat to democracy." Which amounts to a gentle signal, an olive branch of sorts: "Hey cancel culture gods, please listen to us. *We* are with

---

[1] "'Evening With Canceled Women' Gets Canceled," *Reason Magazine* (Published on January 17, 2020. https://reason.com/2020/01/17/evening-with-cancelled-women/. Accessed on November 3, 2020).

[2] "A Letter on Justice and Open Debate," *Harper's Magazine* (Published on July 7, 2020. https://harpers.org/a-letter-on-justice-and-open-debate/. Accessed on November 3, 2020).

you in all the things you hate. But we just want to make sure that others—not us, of course, please don't cancel us—have the freedom to not hate the things that you hate *as much*."

So, did this homage satisfy? Were *Harper's* able to win the audience of the culture of repudiation with their offering? Were they able to propitiate the wrath of those so seldom-pleased gods of cancel culture with this caveat? Not a chance. Their first mistake was not carefully enough vetting the list of signatories of this *free speech statement*, to make sure they were all still free to speak. The signatories accidentally signed this letter against cancel culture alongside other signatories who had been canceled. Within hours of its publication, the apologies and "please-don't-cancel-me's" began to flood the Twittersphere. "I did not know who else had signed that letter," Tweeted Jennifer Finney Boylan, "I thought I was endorsing a well meaning, if vague, message against internet shaming. I did know Chomsky, Steinem, and Atwood were in, and I thought, in good company." She concluded the Tweet with, "The consequences are mine to bear. I am sorry."

Those last three little words are the Twitterfied, lite version of the Communist Show trials in the twentieth century. It is not enough to be punished with dissenting opinions by losing your platform, you have to incriminate yourself by apologizing for your offensive opinions. It does not have to be a heartfelt apology, but it sure better *sound* like it. Say you're sorry. Pay your penance. Offer your sacrificial offering. You have offended the gods of the social system and they must be propitiated.

But what does Orwell and Lewis have to do with Twitter and public shaming? Both *1984* and *That Hideous Strength* foresaw a heavier handed version of cancel culture, and they both, in their ways, warned about it. In fact, *That Hideous Strength* may be a step closer to our situation today, since the totalitarian authority in that story is not a tyrannical state, but rather a subversive group of scientists (or rather, alchemists) and media influencers. But in both cases, insistence on truth eventuates into the same scene: forced reeducation. Here is a glimpse from Orwell.

"That is the world that we are preparing, Winston. A world of victory after victory, triumph after triumph after triumph: an endless pressing, pressing, pressing upon the nerve of power. You are beginning, I can see, to realize what that world will be like. But in the end, you will do more than understand it. You will accept it, welcome it, become part of it." Winston had recovered himself sufficiently to speak.
"You can't!" he said weakly.
"What do you mean by that remark, Winston?"
"You could not create such a world as you have just described. It is a dream. It is impossible."
"Why?"
"It is impossible to found a civilization on fear and hatred and cruelty. It would never endure."
"Why not?"
"It would have no vitality. It would disintegrate. It would commit suicide."
"Nonsense. You are under the impression that hatred is more exhausting than love. Why should it be? And if it were, what difference would that make? Suppose that we choose to wear ourselves out faster. Suppose that we quicken the tempo of human life till men are senile at thirty. Still what difference would it make? Can you not understand that the death of the individual is not death? The party is immortal."[3]

And Lewis:

"You are to conceive the species as an animal which has discovered how to simplify nutrition and locomotion to such a point that the old complex organs and the large body

[3] George Orwell, *Nineteen Eighty-Four*, Oxford World's Classics Edition, Reprint (Oxford, UK: Oxford University Press, 2021), 208–209.

which contained them are no longer necessary. That large body is therefore to disappear. Only a tenth part of it will now be needed to support the brain. The individual is to become all head. The human race is to become all Technocracy."

"I see," said Mark. "I had thought rather vaguely—that the intelligent nucleus would be extended by education."

"That is pure chimera. The great majority of the human race can be educated only in the sense of being given knowledge: they cannot be trained into the total objectivity of mind which is now necessary. They will always remain animals, looking at the world through the haze of their subjective reactions. Even if they could, the day for a large population has passed. It has served its function by acting as a kind of cocoon for Technocratic and Objective Man."[4]

The difference is that in the world of *1984*, one is left to conclude that once illegitimate positions of power have the *de facto* authority to make you apologize for thinking unapproved thoughts, you are too late. Pack it in. You are left between having your face chewed off by rats or saying, "$2 + 2 = 5$." But in the world of *That Hideous Strength*, telling truth is to establish your membership in the winning team. The totalitarians cannot stay at the top, because the top is without of their reach. The heavens sit on top of them; to climb to the top is to pull deep heaven down on top of your head, whereby the tower of Babel crumbles.

During the time of their publication, both novels taught the lesson that we should determine to refuse to cater to untruth. "Live not by lies" was the title of Alexander Solzhenitsyn's final article to the Russian people before his exile to the West.[5] "So in our timidity," he said,

---

[4] C.S. Lewis, *That Hideous Strength* (London, UK: The Bodley Head, 1945), 237–238.

[5] It is also the title of an incredible book by Rod Dreher, *Live Not By Lies: A Manual for Christian Dissidents* (New York, NY: Sentinel, 2020).

let us each make a choice: whether to remain consciously a servant of falsehood (of course, it is not out of inclination but to feed one's family that one raises one's children in the spirit of lies), or to shrug off the lies and become an honest man worthy of respect from one's children and contemporaries....On any given day, any one of us, even those securely working in technical sciences, will be confronted...Either truth or falsehood: towards spiritual independence or towards spiritual servanthood.[6]

Both Orwell and Lewis said, more or less, the same thing some thirty years earlier (before the West really saw what havoc communism had the capacity to wreak), but Solzhenitsyn sounds more Lewisian than Orwellian (which is encouraging because cancel culture itself is closer to a Lewisian nightmare than an Orwellian one). Orwell's story says, "Speak up before speaking up is no longer an option," which is only as potent a message as one's perception of the situation will allow—how do we know when it is no longer an option? But Lewis (with Solzhenitsyn) says, "*Always* speak up. Even if it costs you everything. Telling truth is 'being on the right side of history,' because history is written by the God of all Truth." Christians should be fundamentally opposed to cancel culture because cancel culture traffics in self-deception. The lying team is the losing team.

---

[6] Alexander Solzhenitsyn, "Live Not By Lies," (https://journals.sagepub.com /doi/pdf/10.1080-/0306422-0408537357. Accessed on November 3, 2020).

Chapter 15
Men and Abortion

I am among the ranks of those who were severely convicted in 2015 for having been relatively indifferent towards the scourge of abortion in this country. Like many Christians, I had always been principally "pro-life;" I had liked tweets, shared articles, written Facebook statuses, and engaged in the casual conversation about how wicked it is that we are a country that has slaughtered some sixty-two million humans in a single lifetime. And, like many that year, I was unnerved by the undercover journalism which shined a spotlight on barbaric people doing (big surprise) barbaric acts (namely, selling the severed body parts of murdered infants). I was also unnerved by how unnerved I was at this discovery. The shocking thing about this whole revelation is how shocking it was: what invisible line was crossed to make these actions intolerable? Would it somehow be less barbaric if these hitmen used ultrasound technology to dismember little babies and then threw the remains into the dumpster rather than selling the remains for a profit? Let's be real here, Planned Parenthood didn't get more evil when it decided to get even more bang out of its buck by getting into the business of body snatching, it has always been a human slaughterhouse, which is about as vile as you can get.

So these discoveries forced me into the uncomfortable position of considering how comfortable I was with abortion, so long as it remained behind closed doors. And somehow, I managed to be surprised when this discovery resulted in nearly nothing. Scratch that. It resulted in lawsuits against the brave men and women who decided that the public needed to know the full truth of what was happening behind closed doors, it resulted in Cecile Richards comically contradicting herself for the whole nation to see without any sort of repercussion (as if she were giving every thinking pro-lifer a middle finger and saying, "What are you gonna do?"),[1] and it resulted in the confounding hashtag, #shoutyourabortion. And even more unnerving than all of this, I have found, is the fact that every single one of these realities can leave our minds just as quickly as they entered them, and we can continue to go about our business.

So, I am seeking to foster an abiding dissatisfaction for the fact that abortion still exists. And I have been on the prowl, seeking to stir up the same sort of dissatisfaction with others, in the hopes of attacking the issue on every level, including participating in the simple act of going to abortion clinics to beg women not to murder their babies. I'm not talking about coming with a condemning spirit to shame women; I'm talking about coming with a spirit of gentleness and love, to say, "Please, don't do this. If you are in trouble financially, our church will help you. If you cannot raise your child, someone in our church will adopt him or her. Your problem will not go away if you do this; you will not cease to be a mother, you will only make yourself a mother who murdered her child." I am talking about coming with the whole gospel—unabridged, unemasculated by rhetoric that refuses to call a spade a spade (or a murder a murder)—for women on their way in and for women on their way out.

As I have advocated for this kind of activism, I have been shocked by some of the push-back I have received. Push-back from Christian men, saying, "Sheesh, I don't know if it's such a good idea for men to do that. Maybe we should try to get some of the women in our church to do it instead." Don't get me wrong, I think our message can only stand to be strengthened by having women there, in the parking lot, begging for mercy on behalf of

---

[1] I.e., insisting in one interview that Planned Parenthood provides many services for women, including mammograms, and then swearing up and down that "Planned Parenthood doesn't provide mammograms and we've never said we do" in other interviews.

these babies. Even better still is the prospect of bringing children too. But this impulse that says, "Men should not be there," should be laid to rest. Abortion is a problem for men. Let me offer three reasons why:

Abortion is not a women's rights issue

That is the lie that we have been fed, and we have gobbled it up all too quickly; this "let the women in our churches do it" is what our belch sounds like. No, abortion is not a women's rights issue. It is a societal idolatry issue. It is an indictment on us men when we passively believe the narrative that abortion has nothing whatsoever to do with us. Men were culpable in ancient pagan societies along with the murderous women who brought their babies to the priests of Molech to be sacrificed, and men are culpable now along with the murderous women in our own society who do the same. Men should lie awake at night to know that the society they help to shape is tolerant of human sacrifice. When our culture says, "You're not welcome here, this is a space that pertains to women only, you need to leave," we ought to respond with, "No. I prefer not to stand idly while human beings are being slaughtered, thank you very much."

Abortion is downstream from fatherlessness

Abortions cannot happen without pregnancies, and pregnancies cannot happen without men. What abortion shows us is that men in our society have contented themselves with sowing their seed and walking away. Men in our society are content to use women rather than be spent for them. I recognize that a minority of abortions take place in scenarios where the fathers want to keep their babies, and their mothers decide to kill them anyway. But more often than not, mothers are abandoned—and thereafter hear the lie that they are subsequently justified to rid themselves of their motherhood—or worse yet, mothers are encouraged to murder their babies by the babies' own fathers. How many fathers drive their girlfriends or wives to the abortion clinic to kill their children? How many grandfathers drive their daughters to the abortion clinic to have their grandchildren murdered? Abortion has not become such an epidemic in a vacuum, one of the contributing factors here are men who forsake their responsibilities to die to self in provision for their wives and children, resulting in some sixty-two million infant corpses downstream. It will therefore take men who are willing to assume their responsibilities to die to self in provision for their wives and children—and to work tirelessly for the oppressed and the weak—to swim back upstream in order to see this evil overthrown.

Women need to see what true biblical manhood looks like

Many of the women who are entering into these slaughterhouses have arrived there precisely because they have no prior experience with true manhood. They have experienced men who, instead of self-sacrificially providing for them and protecting them, have used and abused them, and have left them to deal with the consequences of their own selfishness. They have experienced men who would rather see their children murdered than have to forego their self-centered ambitions and indulgences. They have experienced fathers who would rather have their daughters become murderers than have their familial image smeared with a bastard grandchild.

The women in this society need to see what true manhood looks like. They need to see men who own their responsibility to help shape culture properly. They need to see men who recognize that they have a stake in the murder of children as well. They need to see men who are willing to inconvenience themselves by speaking on behalf of those who can't speak for themselves. And daughters need to see this from their fathers: they need to see that a true man is not passive towards injustice. They need to hear the sound of a true man's voice, pleading for the cause of the oppressed. They need to see that abortion is men's problem too.

Speaking and working against the demonic and barbaric act of abortion is not something for which men require permission. They *must* not wait for permission, in fact. Hating such an evil is a prerequisite for righteousness. And while we are on the subject of "prerequisites," let it be known that there is *no necessary* social prerequisite for getting to speak out against abortion. We should decisively put to death that foolish notion that says before objecting to murdering babies under the banner of "pro-life," one must satisfactorily establish "pro-life" status by being on the forefront of orphan care, adoption, refugee ministries, homeless ministries, etc. These things are clearly *consistent* with being "pro-life," but the increasingly common dichotomy of "pro-life" vs. "pro-birth" should be laughed out of the room. How, pray tell, is it possible to be "pro-life" without *first* being "pro-birth?"

This is a smokescreen, and to put the matter plainly, Christians who play along are suckers. The goal-post will always change for what constitutes as caring for enough issues to *get to care* about abortion. Hating "baby-hacking" requires no credentials, especially if those credentials are handed out by those who have no objection to "baby-hacking." Frankly, I'm quite sure I *do not want* the approval of such individuals anyway. They can keep it.

Chapter 16
Transgenderism and
Preferred Personal Pronouns

The apostle Paul was a divider. This is not to say he was against *unity* per se. In fact, in a very real way, you could say that the unity of the Church was one of Paul's hallmarks (Eph. 4:1–7). But the unity Paul was after was *thick*. Much thicker than "politeness" or a shallow sense of getting along. Which is why he had no problem dividing the world up into two kinds of people: those who are in Christ, and those who are in Adam (Rom. 5:12–21). Those who are dead in their trespasses (Eph. 2:1–3), and those who are alive together with Christ (Eph. 2:4–10). Those who view Christ according to the flesh, and those who view him thus no longer because they are "a new creation, the old has passed away, behold, the new has come" (2 Cor. 5:16–17).

And Paul's division doesn't stop there. Not only does he divide humanity in half, he also divides the universe's systemic order in half: "He has delivered us from the domain of darkness and transferred us to the kingdom of his beloved Son, in whom we have redemption, the forgiveness of sins" (Col. 1:13–14). This is a stark distinction: there is a "domain of darkness," and there is a "kingdom of God's beloved Son." Every individual on planet earth is a part of one of these two cosmic orders. We're all born into the former, and some of us are born again into the latter.

And, just like how cultures and subcultures have their own distinct concepts and agendas and ideologies, so too do these respective domains. Just like how the citizens of Christ's kingdom enjoy "the bread" and "cup of blessing," which is our "participation in the body and blood of Christ" (1 Cor. 10:16–17), the domain of darkness has a litany of its own demonic *sacraments*. Paul has to tell the Corinthians that the idolatrous rituals of their neighbors weren't neutral. They were "communion meals" for those in the domain of darkness: "I imply that what pagans sacrifice they offer to demons and not to God. *I do not want you to be participants with demons. You cannot drink the cup of the Lord and the cup of demons. You cannot partake of the table of the Lord and the table of demons*" (1 Cor. 10:20–21, emphasis mine).

How interesting. Paul is telling *Christians* that they ought not "be participants with demons" by blindly participating in the social conventions of their neighbors. In this, he annihilates the myth of neutrality. The agendas that are pushed around in our culture are all coming from *somewhere*. Their genesis is either in the domain of darkness, or the kingdom of God's beloved Son. The many ideas whizzing by us have either been "taken captive to obey Christ," or are "raised against the knowledge of God" (2 Cor. 10:5).

Now that we have the principle sorted out in our own minds, let's apply it to one particular area. Transgenderism: is it an idea arising from the domain of darkness or the kingdom of God's beloved Son? Is it an argument in submission to Christ or is it raised in rebellion against the knowledge of God? To ask the question is to answer it.

"So God created man in his own image, in the image of God he created him; male and female he created them" (Gen. 1:27). No distinction between "gender" and "biological sex" here. God is not silent. "I know my biological sex," I say, "but what is my gender?" And God has spoken: "*XY*." Clear as day, he has answered my question.

Now, up until this point, very few professing evangelicals would object to anything I have said. In fact, some may be getting impatient. *Yeah yeah, that's the easy question, but what about the more difficult one? What about the question that baited us into reading this article?* But this is actually quite important, because we are constructing an argument. And the baseline of this argument is to establish what is *real*. If *God* has spoken "XX" or "XY," then our professed gender is either in submission to his authority, or it is in rejection to it. The adage "he who defines, wins" rings (terrifyingly) true.

So let me answer the question directly, and then, for those who care to read on, let me explain why I believe Christians *must* answer the question this way.

Question: *Should I use my trans neighbor's preferred personal pronoun?*

Answer: No. Christians should not refer to their transgender neighbors by their preferred gender pronouns. And no, I do not think this is a small issue that Christians can simply agree to disagree on. The way you answer this question determines if you have any *integral* and distinctly Christian thing to say about this topic.

What concerns us is not merely what a preferred gender pronoun *is*, but also what it *means*. "XY and *her,* please and thank you," *means* rebellion against God. It means that man, not God, is the measure of all things. It means that man is man's own god, and reality bends to his wishes (or her or zim or sie or em or ver or ter).

God speaks. And in his speech, reality is constituted. He names things as they are, *because* he is authoritative. Defining reality, in other words, is a divine responsibility. *Redefining* reality is therefore creaturely insurrection (Gen. 11:4). "I am XY and *her*" means "God is not God: I am." Further, for us to call an "XY" a "her" also means something. "Sure," it means, "I will reinforce your rebellious delusion. Gender actually *is* something in your control, and is *not* a prerogative of God alone. You may subvert God's created order and be fine."

Now, the reality is that the domain of darkness is a complex society. Not all those who belong to such a domain are equally influential or knowledgeable. Some people in the domain of darkness are captains for worldliness, and some are foot soldiers. What's more, some are non-combatants who are captive to the oppressors of a dark regime. This awareness has led some Christians to mistakenly assume that under the right conditions (say when dealing with a non-combatant), it is acceptable for Christians to acquiesce to their transgender neighbors and call them by their preferred gender pronouns. The argument goes something like this: "some transgender people are not in open, conscious rebellion against God; they are rather confused and deceived by worldly agendas. We should have compassion on them and not unnecessarily offend them." To which I offer my hearty "Amen." But that word "unnecessarily" is important in this instance. If refusing to bear false witness with and for our trans neighbors offends them, it is *necessary* to offend them, for three reasons.

Christians are ministers of reality

Our world thinks up is down and down is up. It calls evil good and good evil. The Christian worldview reorients our conception of reality. The good news of the gospel brings other good news as well: "Good news, we know why you keep shooting up into the air and crashing into the ceiling. It's because you're trying to walk upside down. That's not the ceiling, that's the floor. You didn't shoot up, you fell down. Here's how it actually works." This doesn't mean that Christians must be saying *everything* true about *every sin* at *every moment*. But it does mean that they *must not* lie. So first and foremost, Christians cannot call they "XY" neighbor by any pronoun but "him" because they "XY" neighbor *is* "him" and is *no other pronoun.*

Christians are not to be propagators of godless ideologies

Just like how it was possible for the Corinthians to unwittingly "participate with demons," it is possible for Christians to unwittingly capitulate to godless ideologies. Whenever this happens, it happens little by little, with slight *linguistic* compromises. Our godless society knows this better than we Christians do. This is why "no-fault divorce" was downstream from changing the language of "adultery" to "an affair." And why abortion on demand was downstream from changing "murder" to "pro-choice (or pro-women's health)." And why same-sex "marriage" was downstream from redefining marriage. No longer is it a "sacred institution ordained by God," it is a legal status granted by the state.

On this note, in some regions of society, parents are being urged to stay away from the titles of "mother" and "father." They insist we use, instead, "parent A" and "parent B." (This is particularly big in my wife's field: doula services. Every vestige of "mother" in the literature is being scrubbed and replaced with "pregnant person.") I would venture to guess that most conservative Christians who are fine with adopting alternative gender pronouns for the sake of being "hospitable" will say, "Ok, *that's* crazy. I'd never shy away from addressing *fathers* and *mothers* as such. We draw the line *here*." But I'd venture a guess that those same conservative Christians would have said the same thing about calling a "him" a "her" ten years ago, and yet here we are. Capitulation is a slow-bleed; by it the Christian mission dies the death of a thousand tiny cuts (or tiny linguistic adjustments).

Christians are to be generous, hospitable, and evangelistic

Christians are to be generous and hospitable and evangelistic, and this is why they must not *call their transgender neighbors by alternative pronouns.* This may seem backward, but it makes perfect (gospel) sense if we pause to think about it. The message of the "kingdom of God's beloved Son" and the message of "the domain of darkness" come into necessary conflict. The message of Christianity is peace for the world, but it is not peace with worldliness. This message is offensive by nature. This does not mean that we should labor to be *offensive people*, but it does mean that we should not be afraid to allow our offensive message to offend, because our offensive message is lovingly offensive (may God damn to hell the lie that calls this an oxymoron). This means that the choice of being a "truth-teller" *or* "generous and hospitable" on this question is a false choice. No, we may not *choose* between the two.

Think back on the category distinction I made between "captains of worldliness" on one end, and "non-combatant citizens under an oppressive worldly regime" on the other. Our strategic treatment of an individual will obviously depend on what category they fit into. Sometimes our hands should have boxing gloves on them, and sometimes they should have warm bread *in* them. Sometimes we cut with prophetic edge, and other times we bind with tender care. So yes, we should be "generous" and "hospitable." But, pray tell, is it "generous" or "hospitable" (to either the captain or the non-combatant) for us to signal to them they are right in their opposition to God? Surely not. If we are dealing with a captain, we are passing along ammunition. And if we are dealing with a non-combatant, we are aiding and abetting their oppressors. Which is not generous. They ought to be *liberated* from their oppressors.

The confused teenage boy who comes to your church asking to be called "her" is being co-opted. He's being taken advantage of. He doesn't know that he is being *used* by forces above his head, for an agenda about which he knows nothing. The ideologues who tell him, "You need to call yourself a woman, that will heal what ails you" do not care a lick about him. And you do. So how do you express your love for him? Do you say, "Yes, I agree with your oppressors: I'll play by *their* rules and call you a woman"? That is not love. That sinks the poor lad deeper into the clutches of that dark domain.

Instead, you ought to say, "I can't call you *her* because I actually think it would be unloving for me to do so. You see, you have been told that you are responsible to create your own identity, and to fashion yourself into a gender different from the one God made for you, but that identity is actually much more shallow than the one God has for you. You are *so much more* than that. You have been made in the image of God to be a man, who doesn't live for himself but for God. So instead of reinforcing an identity that I actually think is harmful, can I offer you one that is way better? Way deeper? Way more sacred?"

Here's the painful irony in this whole discussion. We somehow believe that if we simply go along *for a time* with alternative pronouns, we can somehow lessen the blow of what we *actually think* about our neighbor's gender. If we tell *ourselves* that our neighbor's gender is their biological sex, while we refer to *them* by their preferred pronoun, we are speaking out of both sides of our mouths. We are being dishonest. And that is not even pragmatic. The opposite is in fact the case. Not only will the offensive message of the gospel still feel just as offensive three months into the relationship, it will feel worse. "Wait, you think I'm sinning by calling myself a woman? Then why have you been calling me one our entire friendship?!"

We will remain in utter confusion as to what we are supposed to do until we come to grips with the fact that *our message is offensive.* Until we make peace with the fact that there is no way to make our message non-insulting, we will constantly be wringing our hands, trying to figure out the *polite* way to say, "You are a sinner by nature and choice. The identity you've embraced is in opposition to God, and its trajectory is toward hell. Repent of your sinful ways and believe upon the Lord Jesus Christ for salvation." There is no *polite* way of saying that, if by "polite" we mean "non-offensive." But there is always a loving way of saying it. And we ought to say it *that* way.

When we bring our message to the world, "repent and believe the gospel," and our trans neighbor asks in response, "repent of *what?"* Why on earth would we not answer, "well, in part, repent of that sin that you have made central to your very identity"? Some believers ask, "Do we really want to make this issue central to our gospel presentation?" The answer is no. We don't want to make it central to our gospel presentation. But our new-pagan culture has made that decision for us. Central to our gospel presentation is the solution to the problem of sin, and if this sin is central to our hearer's identity, we haven't actually presented the gospel until we've brought it to bear *right ... there.*

Chapter 17

The Christian and Art, Part 1

Christians have a long-standing relationship with the concept of objectivity. Our apologetic efforts are shot through with absolute, objective truth arguments. Our morality hinges on the objective antithesis between *sin* and *godliness*. Our gospel is an objective and exclusive gospel; we believe that there is objectively one Father, and that there is objectively one way for man to reach him—namely, through faith in Christ as the object, whose objective life, death, and resurrection is good news for an objectively fallen humanity. The Bible is our objective standard and final appeal for all belief and practice, and we believe that it is objectively the authoritative, inerrant, inspired word of the Triune God, who, necessarily, objectively exists.

We *love* objectivity. We love absolutes. We love standards, because we know that the world cannot function without them. We also know that those who deny the reality of objectivity in theory contradict themselves in practice. Christians aren't afraid to be counter-culturally objective in the realms of philosophy and morality. We ought not be tempted in the slightest to follow the world's self-defeating, self-destructive endeavors, as her lack of standards in philosophy degenerate into pop-postmodern thought, and her lack of standards in morality degenerate into hedonistic moral relativism. We should not be compelled to blaze that trail with the rest of the world because we can see its bankrupt future.

The world, in its rejection of objectivity, is in serious debt to objectivity. The prolific postmodern author is counting on the objective nature of his publishing contract when he sends his many words (which argue for the subjectivity of words) to his editor; he expects a paycheck with an objective number on it. And the moral relativist betrays his convictions when he wakes up and is objectively outraged to find that his car has been broken into. *What injustice!* We see objectivity in the realms of philosophy and morality—in truth and goodness—well enough, but what about *beauty*? What about *art*?

The world's mutiny against standards has crept in through the church's backdoor; we have believed the lie that beauty in art is, *fundamentally*, subjective. It seems as though we have not deemed the arts an important enough sphere of life to be governed by the lordship of Christ. And when we finally *do* turn to art—in order to consider it through the lens of a Christian worldview—we discover that the way in which we think about art is utterly contrary to the way we think about everything else. We have inherited a standardless conception of art.

But what makes art, *art*? The phrase "beauty is in the eye of the beholder" rolls off the tongue almost instantly. But is beauty truly subjective? "I think this is good art, therefore this is good art"? Now, some readers may be worried about this "slippery slope" I stand upon. I may be thought to be one step away from stodgy old men who sit around and condemn hip-hop. Fear not, those fellows won't hear any cheers from this corner when they furiously *tisk* in the direction of non-classical genres wholesale.

But it is important to note that such men err in having too rigid of a criterion for what constitutes as good art, *not* in their insistence that good art *must have a criterion*. Hip-hop may not by necessity be bad, but there is such a thing as bad hip-hop. When it comes to aesthetics, it's important for us to have different criteria for judging different genres. This is inescapable. We expect one thing when we watch a western and something entirely different when we watch a romantic comedy; we don't expect the same thing from classical music and the blues, or from poetry and a novel. But within all of these categories and sub-categories, we carry a set of objective criteria for judgement. It is possible to have a western film that is objectively garbage because it is possible to have a western film that is pure gold; having the possibility of one necessitates the possibility of the other.

There may be disagreements from person to person about a particular piece of art, and that's where dialogue happens. But dialogue can only happen because some sort of a shared criteria is at least assumed; individuals can only argue about how great or awful a western is because they both assume that an objectively good western is *possible*. There is *such a thing* as a good western.

So genre determines what criteria is used. However, the multiplicity of genres does not—as some might assume—necessitate the legitimacy of all kinds of art; as if wholesale judgments are by necessity off the table. That is simply moving the problem of utter subjectivity one step backwards.

For example, I would argue that pornography is bad "art." It is ugly filmography and ugly photography. Wholesale. And it is bad art, not merely because of the sin that makes up its content (though that is part of it), but also because it is, as a genre, *predicated* on sin. It does not merely have sin in it, it depends on sin to be a genre at all. Every one of the aesthetic effects are *fundamentally* working to beautify something that is ugly; the camera angles and lighting and music and makeup are all working to make sin look beautiful. In other words, the aesthetic element of porn rests on the assumption that sexual sin is lovely, and the genre cannot function as such outside of this basic assumption. The genre fundamentally lies about reality. It uglifies the beauty of the cosmos. So the genre of porn is, wholesale, bad art.

But I would like to go a step further. With respect to visual art, I would say that the abstract impressionism of people like Jackson Pollock could also be judged as ugly. Wholesale. Why? Because of the worldview that it is fundamentally trying to communicate. Porn is a genre that communicates hedonism. So what does randomly splattered paint on a canvas communicate? Nihilism. Chaos.

Allow me to explain how I could be so bold as to pronounce a worldview judgement on a seemingly contentless form of artwork. Content is not the only component of art that matters (or at least, explicitly stated content). Many Christians will readily admit that the truthful content in a hokey Christian film does not excuse its bad character development, bad acting, bad plot, and bad everything else really. Even though the film's content contains truth in it, it is not a good piece of art. Why? Because the other stuff *matters*. You could say it like this: method and style are, in and of themselves, an aspect of *content*.

Let me appear to change the subject for a moment. Creation is fundamentally derivative. God's truth is ultimate and our truth is derivative. God's goodness is ultimate and our goodness is derivative. God's artwork—the work of his hands, his creative craftsmanship, his symphony that he wrote for nature to sing—is ultimate and our artwork is derivative. In other words, God is the only *truly* original artist; all of our artwork is imitation.

As image bearers of God, we cannot escape this; in everything we do, we communicate something about God that may or may not be true. For example, in the same way that man is made in the image of God, marriage is made in the image of the gospel—that is, God's marriage to his people; Christ's marriage to the Church—and every marriage communicates *something* about who God is (even if it misrepresents God). So a faithful husband communicates that Christ is faithful to his Church, and a cheating husband communicates that Christ is unfaithful to his Church; every husband reflects Christ—accurately or inaccurately. And in the same way that man reflects the image of God, and marriage reflects the image of the gospel, so too our art reflects the image of God's art. Subsequently, an artist reflects the image of *the* Artist. And just like it's possible for a marriage to misrepresent the gospel, so too an artist can misrepresent *the* Artist.

Now, think for a moment about God's artwork. Think about the perfectly woven tapestry of nature: every atom has a specific job description, the universe hangs on an unbending skeleton of mathematics, animals and seasons and elements and natural laws and colors and tastes and sounds are all working together like a synchronized dance. Think about the song that creation sings: the birds above the trees take the soprano part, the volcanic core takes the bass, the babbling brooks sing their complex harmonies, exploding stars crash like massive symbols, all while the melody of God's glory booms from church to church. Think about the sunsets he paints with his divine brush: pastels of blue and purple and yellow and grey, contrasting with clouds and oceans and mountains. What do we see when we look at *God's* artwork? We see *intention*. We see *care*. We see *order*.

The finished product tells us something about the Artist. There is a unique and intimate relationship between the Artist and his canvas; he is transcendent, yes (he is not his painting), but he is *breathtakingly* imminent as well.

Now, from looking at this painting, what can we surmise about the relationship between the artist and his canvas?

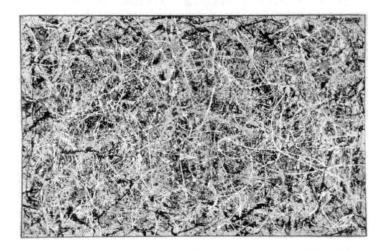

He is removed. He is nonexistent. He is apathetic. His intention is to remove intentionality; the only principle that governs his methodology is *chaos*. He grabs a fistful of dripping paint and chucks it at the wall. He ties a bucket to a string, pokes a hole at the bottom, and lets it swing over the canvas. He lets his paint spill, freely outside of his sovereignty. His purpose is to work with all of his might to *remove* the purpose. For him, there is a very conscientious resistance to the notion that art necessitates intentionality. He wants no providence over his painting.

Now, forget for a moment how intrinsically self-defeating this endeavor is (how intentional do you have to be to remove intentionality?), just notice how antithetical this conception of art is to the Christian worldview. As Christian artists, we strive to reflect the artistic qualities of God. Granted, different genres can express different components of God's artistic qualities, just like how the different genders accentuate his image uniquely. But has God *ever* made a work of art in which he was removed, aloof, and indifferent? Has he *ever* created any masterpiece in which *chaos* was his *fundamental* governing principle? Has he ever operated outside of the realm of intentional, purposeful, providential sovereignty? Absolutely not.

As we move away from these fringe examples of art (hedonistic pornography or standardless postmodern impressionism), the discussion gets more complicated. I don't have an exhaustive list of criteria for judging a work of art, and as we zoom in on particular genres, the discussion gets even more nuanced and more complicated. This may seem intimidating to some, especially because of the unresolved disagreements such a discussion is bound to stir up. But this is one of the ways that we can love the Lord our God with all of our heart, soul, mind and strength.

Chapter 18
The Christian and Art, Part 2

The principle that I tried to lay out in the previous chapter is simple: beauty is defined by conformity to—and reflection of—God. I want to place God not only as the ontological foundation—and thus, criteria—for truth and goodness, but also for beauty. So in the same way that "evil" is defined by its contrast with God's goodness ("evil" is the *ethical* or *moral* equivalent to "not-God-ness"), and in the same way that "falsity" is defined by its contrast with God's truthfulness ("falsity" is the *epistemological* equivalent to "not-God-ness"), I want to say that "ugliness," as an abstract principle, is defined by its contrast with God's beauty ("ugliness" is the *aesthetic* equivalent to "not-God-ness").

Which, as a side note, has serious implications for our beauty-obsessed culture. It means that Christians shouldn't be working to eradicate the category of "ugliness," as is the habit of some, nor should they be seeking to impose the superficial categories of American tabloids for "beauty" and "ugliness," as is the habit of others. Interestingly enough, you can spot both of those positions in different manifestations of the sexual revolution. The former pop up as the "whatever floats your boat" people who stand for revolution by bragging about being the anti-type of a porn-star, and the latter pop up as the Cosmopolitan sex-peddlers who stand for revolution by *securing the careers* of porn-stars. Both groups of people are missing the point; their standards of beauty are too superficial and are hopelessly subjective at the bottom. They need to think *bigger* with the concept of "beauty" in general before they can make their way into the particulars. With both groups, we see the vanity of insisting upon a sexuality-centered identity.

But I digress. What I want to explore right now are two providential levels to which this principle must be applied; namely, the micro-level and the macro-level. Since he's kind of an easy target, I'll keep picking on Jackson Pollock.

At the micro-level, we can identify God's creative craftsmanship in everything—including a Jackson Pollock painting. The fact that God has absolute sovereignty over every square-inch of existence matters. We are *Calvinists* after all; we love that God refuses to let any particle in the cosmos go rogue.

So we see Jackson, in all of his revolutionary thought—his paradigm shifting experiment to annihilate the very notion of sovereignty—take a fistful of dripping paint, and fling it out of his sovereign domain. He lets Mother Nature decide. He lets naturalism take a crack at visual arts. And we, Christians, snicker as God sovereignly and meticulously places a splatter *here* rather than *there*, and another one *here* rather than *there*. *Try again, Pollock.*

No matter how hard he works at it, Jack can never give his paint over into the hands of *chaos*, because *chaos doesn't exist as an entity*. What he's actually doing, on the micro-level, is giving his paint into the hands of divine *providence*—where he starts off to begin with; where he lives and moves and has his being. He throws the paint out of his hands and into God's.

So, on the micro-level of a Jackson Pollock painting, can we identify and appreciate God's creative craftsmanship—his beauty? Answer: we'd better! But this doesn't mean that we must judge the work to be beautiful in and of itself, anymore than a murder carried out with a knife must be judged as a good action on account of God's continual sustaining of the metallic substance of the knife or the heartbeat of the murderer. God's micro-involvement shouldn't be the only defining criteria of the truth, beauty, or goodness of one particular fact; otherwise *every fact of the universe* would be true, beautiful, and good.

But let's take another angle. Let's identify Jack's paintings from the wide-angled lens of God's providence. If all of time and space are God's canvas, then the cosmos and human history can be understood as God's painting. And in this painting, we see creation, fall, redemption, and glorification. We see wholeness, disorder, and repair. We see bright spots and dark contours. We see a lot of *texture*. We see *contrast*. It is a painting that has newborns and mountains and sunsets and laughter, and it also has Hitler and fungi and hurricanes.

If we look *real* close, we can spot Jackson Pollock in his studio, right there with a full ash-tray, a lit cigarette between his lips, and wet paint *all over the place*. He's right *there*, a part of God's painting, and he's making his tiny contribution to the *masterpiece* along with the rest of us.

Now, from this wide-angled lens, can we appreciate Jack's painting and its place in the masterpiece as a whole? Absolutely. But does his contribution equate to *beauty*, in a strictly surface-level sense? Absolutely not. A massive stained-glass window may have a nasty little smudge of grayish-brownish in it, which strictly speaking is "ugly," but which nevertheless contributes to the beauty of the window *as a whole*. So on the grounds of providential placement, I would not want to call Jack's work "beautiful" anymore than I would want to call Saruman's treachery "good," even though it's placement in *The Lord of the Rings* made the story "good."

There's something else that we need to consider as well. I mentioned earlier that artists are imitators; they are what they are by virtue of being image bearers. They are created creators. So when an artist stands in front of a canvas with an idea, he resembles the Triune God in the very act of creation. "*Let there be.*" In the case of Mr. Pollock, I tried to argue that he was a *bad* artist because he misrepresented the *Artist*, and in turn, the true art of reality. Where the *Artist* providentially and meticulously pours care and detail and complexity into his work, Pollock seeks to remove himself entirely. Where the *Artist* employs carefully defined methods to sovereignly piece his creation together, Pollock seeks to adopt chaos and disorder as his governing method. God is the Triune, benevolent Artist to his artwork, while Pollock is, at best, a deistic artist to his.

Now, however, a qualification needs to be made. Though I try to make the case that Pollock is a bad artist because he is a poor representation of *the Artist*, I have to concede the fact that he is still *a* representation. In other words, to some measure, he can't *not* reflect God as an artist. Before he can try to rage against the *Imago Dei* in his artwork, he has to put his canvas on his easel and get his paint out, which will never be any-thing less than an imitation of God spreading out the void in preparation to create his *ex-nihilo* masterpiece. He can't deny the *Imago Dei* without establishing the *Imago Dei*.

So yes, there is some artistic reflection of God in Jackson Pollock's painting, insofar as his endeavor to paint *at all* is a reflection of God. But this qualification is applicable for all people in all things and in all circumstances, because all people and all things and all circumstances are ultimately and ontologically contingent upon God. This applies to the moral relativist and the postmodern philosopher as well. The very fact that the moral relativist even has the desire to engage in the arena of *morality* is a testament to the fact that he is a moral creature, created in the image of a moral God. The very fact that a postmodern philosopher even has the desire to engage in the arena of *rationality* is a testament to the fact that he is a rational creature, created in the image of a rational God.

The simple reality that Pollock's endeavor to create art as a reflection of God should not necessarily lead us to conclude that his artwork is *beautiful*, any more than we ought to conclude that the moral relativist or postmodern philosopher are morally good or rationally right.

We have to pay attention to proportion. If you have a bowl of sugar, and you add a bit of salt, you still have a bowl of sugar. But if you continue to add more and more salt, eventually you will have a bowl of salt, despite the fact that sugar is still in there. Moral relativism, postmodern philosophy, and Pollock's abstract impressionism are bowls of salt, with a little bit of sugar.

Chapter 19
"Pulling Down Deep Heaven:"
On Transhumanism

One of the most curious features of Western society, as it marches on towards the twenty-first century's third decade, is its obsession with the need for more self-esteem. This feature is curious because, while one might assume the obsession is a reaction to a self-esteem deficit, there seems to be no limit for how high modern man thinks of himself. Several signs would indicate that if there is anything he does *not* need any help with, it is self-esteem. One sign of humanity's high-estimation of itself is *transhumanism.* Though many Christians may have never heard the term, the Church does not have the luxury of ignoring transhumanism—the smartphones lining her members' pockets consents her to have the conversation, whether she is ready or not. Precious little interaction with transhumanism has been offered by the Church as of yet (though there are notable exceptions).

What is transhumanism? As defined by transhumanists themselves, it is "a class of philosophies of life that seek the continuation and acceleration of the evolution of intelligent life beyond its currently human form and human limitations by means of science and technology."[1] Stated simply, transhumanism is a proposal to merge technology with humanity to enhance or improve the human condition and experience. Thus, it is "a worldview and is related to other worldviews... It rejects the supernatural (though notes of transcendence echo throughout). Instead, transhumanism emphasizes that we discover meaning and ethics via

---

[1] "What Is Transhumanism?," *What Is Transhumanism* (https://whatistranshumanism.org. Accessed on November 3, 2020).

reason, progress, and the value of existence."[2] This element of rejecting the supernatural is important and distinguishes between
the utility of technological advancements on the one hand, and an
embrace of transhumanism proper on the other. Transhumanism
is fundamentally materialistic: it is the assumption that humanity
will overcome the imposing threat of mortality through natural-
istic means or not at all.

We can understand transhumanism further in relation to its
neighboring concept, *posthumanism*. Transhumanism and
posthumanism relate to one another as the means relate to the
end, or the path to the destination. Michael Plato points out, however, that many posthumanists resent this characterization, insisting that their differences with transhumanism are far more substantial. "Like posthumanism," Plato explains, "transhumanism
explores the space between the human and technology; but, while
posthumanism looks to technology as a means of merging with
the rest of the world and erasing the distinctiveness of the human,
transhumanists see technology as evolution, advancing the cause
of the human, especially human liberation."[3] He goes on to sum-
marize, "In a sense, transhumanism is merely the old humanism
by other means, and for this reason, many posthumanists strongly
reject being correlated with it."[4]

Metaphysically, posthumanism is far more self-conscious than
transhumanism. Whereas transhumanism assumes a bare materialism (i.e., "not supernatural" is about as specific as it gets),
posthumanism intentionally promotes a kind of monism (i.e.,
man is not special, since he is the stuff of the rest of the cosmos
and, therefore, placing a value distinction on him is necessarily
arbitrary). The two distinguish themselves, then, as the

---

[2] Jacob Shatzer, *Transhumanism and the Image of God: Today's Technology and the Future of Christian Discipleship* (Downers Grove, IL: IVP Academic, 2019), 40-41.
[3] Michael J. Plato, "Leonardo DaVinci, James Cameron, and Trans-Species 'Love': The Brave New Vision of Posthumanism," *Permenant Things* 1, no. 1 (n.d.): 10.
[4] Plato, "Leonardo DaVinci," 9.

glorification of the human race through technological measures on the one hand (transhumanism), versus the transcendence and eventual dissolution of the human race through the same measures on the other (posthumanism). We might imagine a conversation between a posthumanist and a transhumanist, in which the posthumanists says something along the lines of, "What makes humanity so special? Give up the idea that humanity matters, let it go." The transhumanist could truthfully respond (though he would not, given his lack of metaphysical awareness) with, "Be patient! What I am doing cannot but end in the abolition of humanity. I'm the one who will give you your desired future."

In one sense, interpreting transhumanism is daunting. Because it boasts of unprecedented technological advancements, with a view toward a future heretofore unimagined, it may appear as though transhumanism evades any possible theological interpretation. As if theology must bow out and concede humanity's growth beyond its relevance. But these brave new ideas are indeed still "under the sun," wherein resides nothing new (Eccl. 1:10). The posthumanism of Braidotti, the transhumanism of Harari, and even the anti-humanism of Foucault may differ from one another in the particulars of their systems, but they all begin from the same place. Each share the same starting point: a resolute declaration of independence from God. Which is to say, they have taken counsel "against the LORD and against his Anointed" in company with the nations who have raged since the earth began groaning (Ps. 2:2–3, cf. Rom. 8:19–20). Thus, transhumanism's cry to overcome creaturely limitations rings with a familiar timbre: "Come, let us build ourselves a city and a tower with its top in the heavens, and let us make a name for ourselves" (Gen. 11:4).

At the heart of Babel's rebellion was self-idolatry. Having been made in the image of God, as creatures covenantally accountable to God to "be fruitful and multiply" (Gen. 1:28; 9:1), Adam's posterity bent all of their God-given ingenuity upon themselves. The

dominion they sought was not as vice regents and obedient wor-
shipers of the living God, but as self-worshiping deities. "Let us
make a name for ourselves, lest we be dispersed over the face of
the whole earth," amounts to "let us worship ourselves, lest we remain accountable to God." Much the same can be said of transhumanism's striving for immortality—in technology they trust.

The relevance of Babel on the present transhumanism discussion is further demonstrated, interestingly enough, by C.S. Lewis.
In the third and final installment of his Sci-fi Space Trilogy novels,
That Hideous Strength, Lewis reimagines the fall of Babel in mid-
twentieth century England. The primary antagonistic organization of the book, the National Institute for Co-ordinated Experiments (N.I.C.E.), touts ambitions eerily similar to the utopian
claims of transhumanism. One sympathizer with the N.I.C.E., for
example, describes the organization's potential in this way: "It
does really look as if we now had the power to dig ourselves in as
a species for a pretty staggering period, to take control of our own
destiny. *If Science is really given a free hand it can now take over
the human race and recondition it: make man a really efficient animal.* If it doesn't—well, we're done."[5] In the course of the novel,
Lewis reveals that beneath its utopian, transhumanistic surface,
the N.I.C.E. smuggles dystopian, posthumanistic ideals. Augustus
Frost, one of the organization's leaders, says,

> You are to conceive the species as an animal which has dis-
> covered how to simplify nutrition and locomotion to such
> a point that the old complex organs and the large body
> which contained them are no longer necessary. That large
> body is therefore to disappear. Only a tenth part of it will
> now be needed to support the brain. The individual is to

---

[5] C.S Lewis, *That Hideous Strength* (New York: Macmillan, 1977), 41. *Emphasis
added.*

become all head. The human race is to become all Technocracy.[6]

Perhaps the most striking feature of this novel is what Lewis portrays as sitting even deeper below the surface: paganism. Lewis believes that demonic forces "press us toward two opposite errors—either to disbelieve in them completely or to develop an unhealthy interest in them. They want to turn us into either materialists or magicians, to encourage us to practice either scientism (which is not the same as science) or the occult. Either will do."[7] In another work of insightful fiction, *The Screwtape Letters*, Lewis imagines a senior demon expressing his desire to tempt humans ("Patients") into becoming a hybrid between the two (i.e., materialism and the supernatural). The product of such a hybrid is "the Materialist Magician, the man, not using, but veritably worshipping, what he vaguely calls 'Forces' while denying the existence of 'spirits.'"[8] "There is something which unites magic and applied science..." says Lewis in *The Abolition of Man*, "For magic and applied science alike the problem is how to subdue reality to the wishes of men: the solution is a technique; and both, in practice of this technique, are ready to do things hitherto regarded as disgusting and impious."[9] Not in vain does the protagonist of Lewis's Space Trilogy, professor Ransom, conclude that "there's no niche in the world for people that won't be either Pagan or Christian."[10]

Toward the conclusion of *That Hideous Strength*, the N.I.C.E. implodes upon itself. Chaos ensues at a banquet with all the movers and shakers of the organization: speech devolves into

---

[6] Lewis, *That Hideous Strength*, 258–259.
[7] Joe Rigney, *Lewis on the Christian Life: Becoming Truly Human in the Presence of God*, Theologians on the Christian life (Wheaton, IL: Crossway, 2018), 85.
[8] C.S. Lewis, *The Screwtape Letters* (New York, NY: Harper Collins, 1996), 31–32.What Lewis here has Screwtape fantasizing about is what he has N.I.C.E. realize.
[9] C.S. Lewis, *The Abolition of Man* (San Francisco, CA: HarperCollins, 2001), 77.
[10] Lewis, *That Hideous Strength*, 351.

gibberish, and sophistication and class devolve into mindless violence.[11] The imagery is powerful: consistent with its own self-destructive ideals, the tower of Babel topples over on itself and God gives "them up in the lusts of their hearts to impurity, to the dishonoring of their bodies among themselves" (Rom. 1:24). They reached for the heavens and "pulled down Deep Heaven on their heads."[12]

Though Lewis's account is fictional, he puts his thumb on the fundamental problem of scientism—upon which transhumanism rests. Any philosophical proposal that declares its independence from God is suicidal. It does not matter if the independence is strictly metaphysical, epistemological, or ethical in nature; any attempt to sever a part of the chord of dependence that binds creature to Creator is an attempt to sever the chord altogether. Transhumanism cannot remain what it is without rejecting the authority of the Creator; to reject God's authority a little is to reject it altogether. Transhumanism views humanity merely as a part of matter, beholden to no one for anything—if matter can be molded to make bricks, why not mold it also to make immortals? Above transhumanists, in their estimation, is only sky. Therefore, the attribute transhumanism pines after is aseity; the authority an ability to be self-existent. But this would be to bridge the chasm between the Creator and his creatures; aseity is an attribute belonging to the Triune God alone.

For "the heavens and the earth" to be ontologically derivative upon God means we can only understand each fact therein, most fundamentally, in its relation to God. No single fact of this universe has existential autonomy—all things are from and through and to the Trinity (Rom. 11:36). God is definitional. Which means that the Creator-creature distinction runs all the way through.

---

[11] Lewis, *That Hideous Strength*, Ch. 16.
[12] Lewis, *That Hideous Strength*, 271.

Squarely on the creaturely side of this Creator-creature divide re-sides man.

Man's being made in God's image is of particular import on the present discussion. Like the rest of creation, his being is deriv-ative upon the creative agency of God, and therefore cannot be defined except in relation to God. Unlike the rest of creation, how-ever, there is a unique breadth and depth to this "relation." As Herman Bavinck points out, "All creatures live and move and have their being in God (Acts 17:28). Animals and plants also stand in relation to God. But in the case of humanity, that relation is a *relationship* and a *post* or *office…* This peculiar human rela-tion to God we call 'religion.'"[13]

The biblical vision of man is therefore high in one sense and low in another. It is high in relation to the rest of the created order, under which God has given him dominion (Ps. 8). It is low in the sense that it views all of humanity firmly on the creature side of the Creator-creature divide. Already then, we see the City of God cannot go along with the City of Man's transhumanism pro-posal—its Babel-tower building project. Christianity's view of man is both too high and too low to shake hands with transhu-manism. Over and against transhumanism's overtly monistic ex-pressions, insisting on the insignificance of humanity to the point of a sneer, the Christian worldview assigns a breathtaking nobility to man. Over and against transhumanism's hubris and trium-phant expressions—most notably in its conquest to overcome mortality—the Christian worldview emphasizes man's funda-mental creatureliness.

Though new in name, transhumanism is rightly understood as Babel's recapitulation in the twenty-first century, and is therefore an expression of the antithesis, and human hubris at its zenith.

---

[13] Herman Bavinck, *Reformed Ethics*, ed. John Bolt, vol. 1: Created, Fallen, and Converted Humanity (Grand Rapids, MI: Baker Academic, 2019), 50.

Therefore, I propose, in brief, the Church responds to the phenomenon of transhumanism in the following ways.

The Church should disciple

First, the Church should disciple her members to understand reality. Crucial here, is the Pastor-theologian's role as a "minister of reality."[14] Transhumanism, as a worldview, catechizes. As it increases in prominence within the wider culture, its catechesis will widen. Already, as sojourners and aliens, citizens of heaven dwelling on earth, Christians receive an education at the hand of transhumanism's subversive pedagogues through entertainment. It is therefore crucial that they receive regular instruction from the biblical worldview to reorient reality and bring every thought captive to obey Christ (2 Cor. 10:5).

Included here is not merely the task of instructing Christians negatively—on what is *not* true about themselves and God and the world; the work of exposing false accounts of reality—but also, and most importantly, the task of instructing Christians positively. This is the work of discipleship—what Kevin Vanhoozer describes as constructing the "Christian imagination," in his recent work, *Hearers & Doers: A Pastor's Guide to Making Disciples Through Scripture and Doctrine*.[15] "True disciples," insists Vanhoozer, "are awake and alert to what is going on in the world, to what is really real, namely, the 'real presence' of Jesus Christ. The true story of the world, narrated in Scripture, concerns God's presence and activity."[16]

Christians will recognize the counterfeit gospel of transhumanism—with its non-reality of "redefining humanity"—only

---

[14] I am borrowing this concept from Kevin J. Vanhoozer and Owen Strachan, *The Pastor as Public Theologian: Reclaiming a Lost Vision* (Grand Rapids, MI: Baker Academic, 2015). See also, Kevin J Vanhoozer, *Hearers & Doers: A Pastor's Guide to Making Disciples through Scripture and Doctrine* (Bellingham, WA: Lexham Press, 2019).

[15] See, Vanhoozer, *Hearers and Doers*, 85.

[16] Vanhoozer, *Hearers and Doers*, 54.

when they internalize and indwell the true gospel—with its reality of an *ex nihilo* creation, which is, and always will be, what God declares.

Respond with prophetic witness

Second, the Church should respond to the world with prophetic witness. Those who belong to the Lord Jesus Christ know what happens at Babel. The Church knows that the conquest to overcome mortality as autonomous, self-made deities is a suicidal fool's errand. She knows that humanity is what God says it is, and that it cannot be reinvented or refashioned to "merge with" non-humanity in any ontological fashion. She also knows where the deep drive for immortality comes from (Eccl. 3:11), and where it is found (Jn. 6:54). Therefore, the Church should lovingly and prophetically confront transhumanism's false gospel, exploit its thirst for immortality, and counter-offer with a gospel that can actually make good on its promises (2 Cor. 5:4–5). Transhumanism—along with any other expression of monistic paganism—invests all identity-capitol in a secularist racket. Its foundational notion of reality does not comport with the world as it really is, which means it cannot deliver on its promises. It will leave many a transhumanist bankrupt. Therefore, "Christians must be prepared to minister to the wounded, the refugees of the secular moral revolution whose lives have been wrecked by its false promises of freedom and autonomy."[17]

Showcase gratitude

Third, the Church should showcase gratitude. Christians ought not be alarmists when it comes to technology. The flurry of technological advancement is indicative of human intellect, which is a

---

[17] Nancy Pearcey, *Love Thy Body: Answering Hard Questions About Life and Sexuality* (Grand Rapids, MI: Baker Books, 2018), 264.

gift from God intended for his glory in the task of dominion-taking (Gen. 1:28; Mk. 12:30; 1 Tim. 4:4; 1 Cor. 10:31). A robust embrace of divine providence and common grace allows Christians to receive technological progress as a gift from the Father of lights (Jas. 1:17). This does not mean that all technological advancements are neutral and harmless. Indeed, some are intrinsically more dangerous than others. Yet dangerous gifts need not be wholesale rejected. A power-drill is more dangerous than a t-shirt, though both may be gifts.

A posture of prophetic gratitude is crucial for Christians in this transhumanism moment. Such a posture orients reality for the Christ aright. It recognizes God enthroned as the sovereign gift-giver, who gifts his image-bearing creatures with technological wonders they ought to receive with thanksgiving, and employ in the service of worship. Christian gratitude is thus a grid through which technological proposals run: that which disorients this order—that which attempts to blur the Creator-creature distinction (or, the distinction between man and his technological gifts)—is to be rejected. The City of God should build—even using the same bricks and mortar the City of Man uses, since they are found in God's world—but it should steer clear of the City of Man's capital tower: Babel. That crowning achievement is structurally unsound and can only wobble for so much longer before it falls.

Chapter 20
The Virtue of Protestant Catholicism

"I do not mean the Church as we see her spread out through all time and space and rooted in eternity, terrible as an army with banners." These are the words C.S. Lewis gave to his character, Screwtape, imagining what a senior demon might think about Christ's one, holy, catholic, apostolic Church. "That," adds Screwtape with a disdainful shudder, "I confess, is a spectacle which makes our boldest tempters uneasy."[1]

This Church—the one spread out through all time and space and rooted in eternity, terrible as an army with banners—is what we confess to believe in when we affirm the Nicene Creed. Not only do we confess to believe in it, we confess also to be a part of it. To be a Christian is necessarily to be a footman in this army; to march behind a sea of faithful warrior-saints who have gone before us, and in front of many who will follow—all on our way to storm the wobbling gates of hell (Matt. 16:18). Of course, this description of the Universal Church, romantic though it sounds, is hard to square with the week by week experience of most local churches. What hath Nicaea to do with the struggling First Baptist Church of *Middle-of-Nowhere*? And more broadly, what does catholicity even mean for Nicene-affirming Protestants? So long as a conflation between "spiritual unity" and "structural unity" remains, a *Protestant-Catholic* is nothing short of an oxymoron.

It is very tempting to pine after an era of the Early Church marked by ultra-unified structure; the golden days when polity was completely and totally uniform. But, alas, such a picture is likely a historical fiction. It took a while before Rome consolidated

---

[1] C.S. Lewis, *The Screwtape Letters*, Reprinted Ed. (New York, NY: HarperOne, 2015), letter 2.

formal authority, and until that point, Nicaea functioned as a doctrinal ballast for the Christian Church. It was understood by those who affirmed it as a codification of the "Rule of Faith"—the "faith once for all delivered to the saints" (Jude 3)—which means that the "oneness" and "catholicity" its proponents defended was not the kind of "oneness" and "catholicity" many of our Roman Catholic friends defend today. It was rather a convictional "oneness," which means it is just as much a part of Protestant (and, dare I say, *evangelical*) heritage as it is a Roman Catholic or (big "O") Orthodox heritage. This is why Protestants can confess the "apostolic" line in the creed with no guile. We affirm an "apostolic succession" of a kind, though it may be better to describe it as a "apostolic foundation," from which we never move beyond (Eph. 2:20–21). "Oneness" in the Nicaean sense, need not imply an absolute structural or relational oneness.

None of this is to imply that structural or relational unity is *unimportant*. Indeed, the spiritual "oneness" that all true Christians share is ample motivation to pursue as deep a unity as possible; bitter factions are manifestly un-Christian. At least, they ought to be; for we are painfully aware that even if sectarianism is un-Christian as a *prescription*, it is all-too-Christian as a *description*. The presence of factions can be spotted all the way back in the New Testament Church (1 Cor. 3:1–9); the tribalism Protestants (sometimes rightly) get a bad rap for, has had to be confronted and rebuked in the Church for two thousand years.

This means that Christ's prayer for his disciples' unity (Jn. 17:20–21), while implying a great deal for how Christians *ought* to act toward one another, nevertheless speaks to a deeper oneness— a spiritually essential oneness that transcends the visible divisions, despite the best efforts of some. Otherwise, Christ's prayer is in fact ineffectual, and held hostage by *our* actions (a dreadful thought). No, Christ has torn down the dividing wall of hostility, and sinfully try as we may to re-erect it, we will ultimately be unable (Eph. 2:14–22). Therefore, just as how all Christians are "holy" in an already/not yet sense—positionally holy in Christ, progressively holier in the present age—so too are all Christians "one" in an already/not yet sense. And just like how the Church's positional holiness ought to motivate her progressive holiness, so too should her positional, eschatological oneness motivate a relational oneness in the present age.

Rather than trying to undo the unifying work of Christ, all Christians—that is, the "one body" brought about by the "one Spirit" and called to the "one hope," under the authority of the "one Lord," who profess the "one faith" expressed in the "one baptism," to the glory of the "one God and Father" (Eph 4:4–5)—ought to recognize their unity in Christ.

Does this then mean an "end of Protestantism?" Not at all.[2] For one thing, we can't stop protesting because none of Rome's dogma of yesteryear, which forced the hand of our Reformed forbearers, has yet been amended or corrected. By all accounts, the theological distance between Rome and "her rebellious children" (as Hans Küng put it) has not narrowed, but only grown. Even if this were not the case, "ending Protestantism" would still be a mistake, since it would necessarily assume that "increasing oneness" amounts to "increasing Romishness." It would assume, in other words, that "oneness" has a scent and sound, which is the smells and bells of Rome. I can't imagine why Protestants should all of a sudden flip the script and start arguing *with* Roman Catholics that Rome is the one true Church.

All this to say, the decision to move *with* the grain of Christ's cosmic Church unity, and not against it, should not look like Protestants rushing to pick up a rosary. Nor should it look like

---

[2] For anyone with ears to hear, this is obviously a cheeky jab at Peter Leithart and his book, *The End of Protestantism: Pursuing Unity in a Fragmented Church* (Grand Rapids, MI: Brazos Press, 2016). I should like to add that as a big admirer of Leithart, I mean no disrespect by my disagreement with his strategy for oneness here.

attempting to find the least common denominator. A thin ecumenism is a weak and brittle ecumenism. Instead of collectively agreeing to climb out of our denominational entrenchments to try to find a ground wide and level enough to fit everyone on, we should stay where we are and begin *digging*. And no, we shouldn't dig just deep enough so that the top of our trench puts everyone else out of view—isolation isn't the goal. We should keep digging, further and further down. If we do, we will ultimately hear the happy *clank* of our shovels hitting each other as we reach our common core. The ecumenism we should strive after, in other words, is not a thin horizontal ecumenism, but rather a thick vertical one; our "common ground," the place where we recognize our oneness, is not on earth's crust, but at its core. And there, like a bush ablaze but not burning, the words of the Nicene Creed invite us to rally around them.

There will, of course, come a day when this "already/not yet" unity will shed its "not yet" description, and the Universal Church's transcendent oneness will immanentize. In that day, the common ground won't be limited to the core, but will extend out to the crust of the New Earth. If we keep this in mind, we can avoid the temptation to either minimize or exaggerate our differences. It will not surprise me in the least, for example, to find brothers and sisters in Christ walking around that glorified Earth who were *Presbyterians* in this age. Though I am convinced that many of them will have been sprinkled in the Triune name, but never formally baptized rightly, I do not doubt that there is nevertheless a Spiritual baptism we share in common (Rom. 6:1–4). In fact, shocking though it may sound to some, I suspect the New Earth will be home to more than a few heavenly citizens who were Roman Catholics in this life, who managed to arrive despite their Church's teaching on justification.

This eschatological, "already/not yet" vision helps us to answer the question I raised above: what hath Nicaea to do with the struggling First Baptist Church of Middle-of-Nowhere (let's call her FBCM)? The answer is that the Universal Church described in the Nicene Creed only becomes visible here and now in local churches, like FBCM. The moment our triune God saves a sinner by grace, the sinner has been enlisted in Christ's cosmic army (though it is true enough that some prefer to go awol).

There are, in point of fact, no *truly* "lone wolf" Christians. A Christian is one who is baptized by the Spirit into "one body" (1 Cor. 12:5), delivered "from the domain of darkness" and transferred into "the dominion of [God's] beloved Son" (Col. 1:13), and a "living stone" who is, together with other Christians, being "built up as a spiritual house, to be a holy priesthood, to offer spiritual sacrifices acceptable to God through Jesus Christ" (1 Pet. 2:4–5).

To be a Christian is to be a member of the One, Holy, Catholic, and Apostolic Church, because God is in the business of binding and loosening *in heaven*. But how does that which is bound and loosened in heaven become bound and loosened on earth? Who is responsible for declaring and legitimizing the new member's status in the Universal Church? To whom does Christ hand his keys to the Kingdom, in order to bind and loosen on earth that which is bound and loosened in heaven (Matt. 16:18–19; 18:15–20)? Local churches like FBCM.

The Church is the Bride of Christ; a people from every tribe and tongue and nation, who have been elected from the foundation of the world, and purchased by the blood of Jesus. This Universal Church is made visible in local churches, and *only* in local churches. Her members are certainly present all over the place, but you can't *see* her until local churches gather. Without little churches like FBCM, talk of the Universal Church would be vacuous. The concept remains phantasmal and ghostly until incarnated with bodies, bread, wine, water, and Word.

Our unimpressive little assemblies are the image of the invisible Church, and whether local churches realize this or not, they are in the same family tree as the fourth century fathers who produced the Nicene Creed. In *our* lineage are figures like Athanasius and Nicholas (who, *unfortunately*, probably never gave Arias a wallop, but if it helps the rumbling, tumbling farmer who serves as a deacon at FBCM to value protestant catholicity a bit more, I say we keep the legend going). Our churches lose something major if we lose this sense of family history.

It is a great irony that the classic fundamentalist creed, "no creed but the Bible," places the liberal-theology-fearing church in danger of losing biblical fidelity. It is no accident that an antipathy for tradition and a crude biblicism lead so often to aberrations to central doctrines like the Trinity, or divine simplicity. The fruit of Nicene Trinitarianism is the product of a particular kind of tree— a way of reading Scripture with roots deep in a specific metaphysic and tradition. Once those roots are cut, we shouldn't expect to see the same kind of fruit.

Out of a protestant love for *Scripture*, then, our local churches should be (small "c") *catholic*. Which is to say, our local churches should stop imagining that they popped up in a vacuum. They should come to recognize who they *are;* to the degree that they are in fact churches, they are a part of the One, Holy, Catholic and Apostolic Church, and they only stand to benefit from waking up to this fact. It is not inconsequential that "catholic" and "apostolic" are placed next to one another. It is downright silly to expect the latter without the former.

But at the end of the day, there is a sense in which local churches are "catholic" whether they like it or not, and there's not a thing they can do about it (short of apostasy). Little sectarian churches, riddled with sin, myopic and factionist, are, mysteriously, the visible expressions of the One, Holy, Catholic, and Apostolic Church. It is astounding, and just like God and his subversive ways, to send this "terrible army" on the march armed with nothing more than a book, water, cheap wine, and stale bread. Somehow, though, this is fittingly foolish (1 Cor. 1:18–31) for a community that proclaims how death was killed by Life, when Life was killed by death (1 Cor. 2:8).

Chapter 21
Natural Theology and
the Tragedy of Chronological Snobbery

The older I get, the more often I find myself coming back to the wisdom of C.S. Lewis. For those who have been immersed in his writings for years, his ever-relevance produces a renewable sense of amazement. He seems to speak out from his mid-twentieth-century grave directly to so many of our pressing questions. *Retributive or distributive justice? Gender complementarity or gender liberation? Education as career preparation or education as virtue formation? Hierarchy or "equity?" The curious mixture of paganism and scientism or Christianity and science? Is the cosmos beyond this world "outer space" or is it "the heavens?"* And, relevant to this post, *the critically appropriated metaphysic of Christian-Platonism or the uncritically assumed metaphysic of Hegelianism.* I am convinced the secret to Lewis' constant prescience is his timelessness. This timeless approach can be summed up in the grave warning to avoid "chronological snobbery"—the *stickiest* of his coined phrases.

I recently listened to a lecture on Thomas Aquinas and Natural Theology that, if it were possible, made my affections for Lewis rise even more. Lewis gets the credit for my attendance in this lecture, in fact. I knew the scholar had a different take on Aquinas than I did, and I entertained the idea of rejecting the invitation to attend. But then I thought, "What would C.S. Lewis do?" He would likely attend with an open mind, ready to engage to the best of his ability, and probably follow up with a written piece engaging with the lecture's content. So, here we are.

Lewis didn't just get me to the lecture, though. He kept coming up throughout. Not by the speaker, but in my mind, almost in conversation with the speaker. I would like to believe that I gave the speaker a fair shake, but when Aristotle and Aquinas were cast as proto-Enlightenment thinkers, locked and loaded with Empiricism-like methodological commitments, I confess I was unable to keep the question of anachronism at bay. And when a supposed thread began to develop between Aristotle, Aquinas, Descartes, Locke and (for the kicker) *Marx*—the thread being the claim that all of these men are examples of what happens when you detach your epistemology from revelation; that sticking with Aristotle will consistently get you to godless therapy and contemporary "woke social justice"—the booming voice of that Oxford don thundered through my head, "*This* is a stunning display of chronological snobbery. *Bless me, what do they teach them at these schools?*"

Now, far be it for me to question the sincerity of this said lecturer. I am sure he is an earnest, faithful brother in Christ, and I don't doubt him when he assured me that he read the *Summa* five times, or when he said he has consulted the major Thomistic scholars of the past couple centuries. But those facts in themselves don't offer any assurance that chronological snobbery is out of his reach. In fact, it was hard to avoid the conclusion that chronological snobbery was at work the way Aquinas was patted on the head, in patronized fashion, "He was a *very brilliant* man... the poor fellow just couldn't start at the right place."

Upon further inspection, however, the primary charge just would not stick. The charge, if I could sum up the point of the talk, was that Aquinas attempted to know God apart from the foundation of revelation. And no, said the speaker, you cannot call Aquinas's pursuit of natural theology an investigation of general revelation. This is because the speaker's definition of general revelation requires immediacy—people know that there is a God, and they suppress the truth about him in unrighteousness (Rom. 1:18). God, the audience was reminded, has made himself known:

"his invisible attributes, namely, his eternal power and divine nature, have been clearly perceived, ever since the creation of the world, in the things that have been made. So, they are without excuse" (Rom. 1:20).

The problem is, I don't see Aquinas disagreeing with the insistence that God's self-revelation in nature renders man's unbelief inexcusable. That is the whole point of natural theology: if God has made himself known in nature, it would seem that certain things about him must be deducible from nature. The hang-up seems to be on this term "immediacy." It is certainly true that Aquinas would reject the notion that all human beings are born pre-loaded with a complete knowledge of God apart from experiencing his self-revelation in nature, but then so would the aforementioned speaker. In fact, after the talk was over, and I engaged the speaker on this very topic, he granted that the immediacy of general revelation—whatever he *does* mean by it—doesn't imply that we fail to experience this revelation through our senses and rationality. It is true that God reveals himself through day and night (Ps. 19:1–6), but that at least implies that getting the message requires the minimum of experiencing *one whole day.*

Aquinas seems to be saying no more and no less about what one can deduce from natural theology than what this lecturer claimed could be learned from general revelation: namely, enough knowledge about God to condemn unbelievers, but not enough to save them. So, how is Aquinas's employment of reason as an effort to grapple with the nature of God via contemplation of the "things that have been made" different than an effort to understand general revelation? I cannot come up with an answer. The best I can do is guess that it has something to do with the presence of a formal syllogism, and too much language about "reason."

What's going on here? As much as it pains me to say it, I have to blame one of my heroes, Cornelius Van Til. It is difficult for me to articulate how much appreciation I have for this saint: Van Til came along at a formative point of my life and effected one of those paradigm-shifts that the average person receives only a handful of times. The chief insight he brought to light was the all-important fact: *neutrality is a myth*. He was absolutely right when he confronted the evidentialist apologists of his day with the hypocrisy of their presuppositions. When you try to step into a world of epistemological neutrality, you are actually stepping into the world of skepticism. The unbeliever doesn't disbelieve because he doesn't have the evidence he requires; he disbelieves because he has a rebel heart. Letting the skeptic determine what constitutes as legitimate evidence for belief is to concede the debate from the outset—because of his makeup as covenant-breaking rebel, he will *always* rig the rules of engagement to leave the Christian God—the Triune God—off the table as a viable conclusion to the argument. It's a foregone conclusion.

The problem is that Van Til took that criticism and started shooting it off in every direction. According to Van Til, "early Christian theologians...all too frequently did not realize that once they agreed that their notion of incomprehensibility of God was the same, in effect, as the idea of the namelessness of God as held by the Greeks, the Gnostics and Plotinus, that then they could logically be compelled to deny the whole of the significance of the appearance of Christ in history."[1] Even more specifically, "Augustine does not realize that in defending a bare theism, a theism alike acceptable to Christians and to non-Christians, he is precluding the possibility of going on to a defense of Christianity."[2] Van Til insists that the same error is inexplicably repeated down through the ages, not the least by Aquinas (one has to remind oneself that Van Til *did not actually believe* he was the first and only consistent

---

[1] Cornelius Van Til, *A Christian Theory of Knowledge* (Phillipsburg, NJ: Presbyterian & Reformed Publishing Company, 1961), 150.

[2] Van Til, *A Christian Theory of Knowledge*, 120.

Christian theologian after Paul, contrary to the impression he occasionally gives).

The whole notion of "Aquinas as proto-Enlightenment thinker" is something Van Til himself entertained and propagandized. "Thomas," insists Van Til, "presents us with a sort of pre-Kantian deduction of the categories."[3] This was inevitable for Aquinas whose "*uncritical* assumption [of Aristotle]... vitiates the entire argument for the existence of God that he offers, and in fact vitiates his approach to every other problem in philosophy and in theology,"[4] since, according to Van Til, "we cannot start with Aristotle without eventually falling prey to Kant."[5] Consequently, anyone who voices appreciation for Aquinas on natural theology is *de facto* guilty of the same intellectual mistake. This is why he cannot close his seminal work, *The Defense of the Faith*, without implicating Warfield and even Bavinck in this Enlightenment-like reliance on rationality: "It is this ever and everywhere present face of God [in general revelation] that Descartes virtually denied when he made the human self the ultimate starting point in predication. This was forgotten by the old Princeton Apologetics; it is also, for the moment, forgotten by Bavinck when he would start with the *cogito* as such as the foundation of human knowledge."[6]

This tunnel vision is frustrating for those of us who appreciate Van Til's conceptual insights in the abstract, but who believe he misses the mark on their application in the particulars. For example, reading his essay, "Nature and Scripture" gives the experience of whiplash. Its first half is a harrowing description of general revelation—the kind of thing that I believe the old theologians of the

---

[3] Cornelius Van Til, "Nature and Scripture" in *The Infallible Word: A Symposium by the Members of the Faculty of Westminster Theological Seminary*, ed. Ned Bernard Stonehouse and Paul Woolley, 2nd ed. (Phillipsburg, NJ: Presbyterian and Reformed Publishing 1967), 291.

[4] Van Til, "Nature and Scripture," 173 (*emphasis mine*).

[5] Cornelius Van Til, *The Defense of the Faith*, 3rd ed. (Phillipsburg, NJ: Presbyterian and Reformed, 1967), 135.

[6] Van Til, *The Defense of the Faith*, 293.

Great Tradition would eat up, and take as an invitation to engage in natural theology to the glory of God. But when he turns his attention to critiquing natural theology in the essay's second half, he anachronistically forces the old theologians' natural theology-talk into the epistemological naturalism of Enlightenment thinkers and burns their whole project to crisps. The fact is, they would see much of themselves in his positive description of general theology, and would scratch their heads at his description of their supposed revelation-less epistemology. They believed in an enchanted cosmos that pulsated with revelation. Man, for them, was no blank slate, nor was he a ghost in the machine: he was a *creature*. Natural theology, for the best of the Great Tradition, was always "faith seeking understanding."

This problem of reducing virtually all non-Van Tilians to Enlightenment thinkers has been made doubly difficult when you consider the fact that epistemological naturalists like William Lane Craig *agree* with Van Til that Aquinas was a kind of proto-Lockean, and celebrated it! This eventuated in the muddled situation that many are trying to sort out right now: someone like William Lane Craig can deny the doctrine of divine simplicity, conceptualize the Trinity in near-tri-theistic fashion, rip Anselm out of his historical context, and own the title of a *classicist*. Meanwhile, Van Til and his followers look at someone like Craig and justly decry his whole project, but not without also decrying the classical tradition because they *agree with him* that he—and others like him—really are genuine inheritors of the classical tradition! And all the while, the *actual* Great Tradition is talked *about* but seldom engaged *with*.

Under this conception, it seems we must choose between the metaphysics of the Great Tradition or the soteriology of the Reformed Tradition, but that we may not have both. Is it possible to harmonize the Great Tradition's metaphysic of "participation" with a Reformed soteriology? Answering this question clearly is certainly not made easier by the fact that some within the Reformed camp agree with the harsh choice between the metaphysic of the Great Tradition and the soteriology of the Reformed tradition.

But is the option truly that stark? Must we decide between embracing the metaphysics of the Great Tradition, and consequently own a Roman (or even an Eastern Orthodox) soteriology, or embracing the Reformed soteriology and, with a heavy and reluctant heart, bid farewell to the gorgeous metaphysic of Christian-Platonism and settle in with the drab and colorless metaphysic of nominalism? Fortunately, no such choice is necessary, because those who would have us choose are mistaken to do so. It is, for one thing, a historically novel choice, since, as Steven Duby notes, "the early Reformed certainly drew on the resources of medieval philosophy and theology in an eclectic manner," but "essentially stood in continuity with Thomas's approach [to metaphysics] and criticized Scotus's doctrine of univocity," and, we might add, nominalism.[7] In fact, Richard Muller's career—indeed his entire project!—has been spent proving the same (see his *Post-Reformation Reformed Dogmatics*).

The fact is, an epistemology of revelation (which is something that I—and I think *Aquinas*, for that matter—want to affirm) requires a metaphysic of realism. We can get that metaphysic from the Great Tradition if we would but receive it with gratitude and humility. This metaphysical realism comes to us from Plato, through Aristotle, through Medieval scholasticism, and is received by the post-Reformation scholastics and Puritans. This means that Van Til and many of his followers, including the lecturer who inspired this post, are not unlike Elijah, self-segregated and thinking themselves the few who remain jealous for the LORD. The invitation is for such individuals to look up and see a

---

[7] Steven J. Duby, *God In Himself: Scripture, Metaphysics, and the Task of Christian Theology* (Downers Grove, IL: IVP Academic, 2019), 257.

cloud of witnesses from the Great Tradition—to be reminded that God has, so to speak, preserved "seven thousand in Israel, all the knees that have not bowed to Baal, and every mouth that has not kissed him" (cf., 1 Kings 19:9–18).

The kind of authority the aforementioned speaker (rightly) insists we render to divine revelation (special and general) is made sense of only in the kind of metaphysic the same speaker rejects in his fundamental denunciation of Aquinas and the Great Tradition. Within this metaphysic, the cosmos pulsates with life and meaning. Creation is good because it is formed in the good mind of the all-good God. The material universe is not good *despite* its physical form; its physical form is *itself* good. But its physical form does not exhaust its essence. The cosmos *means* more than it is.

To come full circle, we see this metaphysic illustrated well by one of Christianity's most widely recognized Christian Platonists (though he is seldom recognized *as such*), C.S. Lewis. He illustrates the point in a conversation between the Narnian star, Ramandu, and Eustace Scrubb in the fantasy classic *The Voyage of the Dawn Treader*:

> "In our world," said Eustace, "a star is a huge ball of flaming gas."
> "Even in your world, my son, that is not what a star is but only what it is made of."[8]

Lewis goes on to make explicit that his Narnian cosmology is Platonic in *The Last Battle*, when earth and Narnia are shown to be expressions of the "further up, further in" reality of Aslan's country. It is Professor Digory who sums up the philosophical point with one last lesson for the Pevensies and their friends:

---

[8] C.S. Lewis, *The Voyage of the Dawn Treader* (New York: NY, Harper Collins, 2002), 115.

Listen, Peter. When Aslan said you could never go back to Narnia, he meant the Narnia you were thinking of. But that was not the real Narnia. That had a beginning and an end. It was only a shadow or a copy of the real Narnia, which has always been here and always will be here: just as our own world, England and all, is only a shadow or copy of something in Aslan's real world. You need not mourn over Narnia, Lucy. All of the old Narnia that mattered, all the dear creatures, have been drawn into the real Narnia through the Door. And of course it is different; as different as a real thing is from a shadow or as waking life is from a dream." His voice stirred everyone like a trumpet as he spoke these words: but [then] he added under his breath "It's all in Plato, all in Plato: bless me, what do they teach them at these schools!"[9]

Within this kind of gratuitous cosmology, wherein the referent of any created thing is not the thing itself, but its God, meaning transgresses the boundaries of all creaturely subjects and find their home in the ultimate Subject. Everything is revelation, and thus contemplation of the relationship between the world and its Maker is the furthest thing from fruitless speculation. It is the full-bodied embrace of *reality*.

---

[9] C. S. Lewis, *The Last Battle*, rev. ed. (New York: HarperCollins, 1994), 211-212.

Chapter 22
Confess Your Disturbing Impulses Here

What constitutes as a sin? This is a question Christians are often occupied with for a number of reasons—some noble, some innocuous, and some suspect. Where, for example, is the line for sexual sin drawn? Is it the physical act of viewing porn or engaging in a sexual act outside of covenant marriage? Is it the mental act of contemplating, fantasizing, or imagining? Or is it in the desire to sin itself—in other words, once the temptation has been aroused, has one sinned? The immediate benefit of drawing the line as close to the physical action as possible is that the genuinely struggling, plodding, fighting Christian, who hates that he is tempted, is not shamed or embarrassed or condemned for feeling impulses he does not wish to feel. The benefit of drawing the line closer to the realm of desire, however, is that that's where the Bible draws it (Js. 1:14).

This, I trust, clears up any confusion about my own conviction on the matter. Sin, I maintain, ought to be defined not only in terms of physical action, but in the desire itself. However, speaking as a pastor and a friend and an experienced sinner, I sympathize with the concern of those who want to define sin in terms of action out of a sensitivity to those who already feel shame for their sinful desires. Minimizing Christian self-condemnation for sins that have been nailed to the cross of Christ is a noble and Christ-honoring aspiration. But the *way* in which this is accomplished matters. We need not choose between minimizing the sinfulness of sin on the one hand, and paralyzing struggling Christians with piling up condemnation and shame on the other. We should both call sinful desires *sinful*, and also create an environment where sinful desires can be freely and openly confessed without shame or condemnation. And the way we do this is by getting our ontology right: we have to understand what sinful desires are in relation to our humanity. To settle this tension, we go to that great doctrine: union with Christ.

Even if you are not willing to define the desire to sin as an *act* of sin, it is difficult to imagine how you could get around calling a desire to sin (forgive the redundancy) *a sinful desire*. Are *sinful desires* not desires to lament over and grieve over and confess? Of course they are. The desire to be contrary to what God has called us to be can hardly be regarded with hospitality for the self-conscious Christian. Such desires reveal a sin-nature (a term that can be admittedly deceptive) that *naturally* does not jive with God. Christians should feel nothing less than *hatred* for such desires. Indeed, there is an appropriate place, even, for *shame*—shameful desires should feel shameful in a sense, even if they should never occasion self-loathing and condemnation.

However one chooses to do it, one must give some account for this *sin-nature*. Perhaps you do not want to call it a sin-nature, because in Christ, the old self has been crucified (Rom. 6:6), sin will no longer have dominion over the Christian (Rom. 6:14), and the Christian is a new creation (2 Cor. 5:17). Well and fine. Give it another name if you don't want to call it "sin-nature." Sinful desires for the believer still come from *somewhere within*. Satan does not implant sinful desires in the hearts of believers. So what do we do with this *from-within-source-of-sinful-desire* (for brevity's sake, I think I will stick with *sin-nature*)? Since it lies within, doesn't that make it basic to our humanity? Doesn't that make it essential to our *ontology*?

The answer is no. This sin-nature is a parasite to human ontology. It is an intruder. It is an unwelcomed guest that has settled so deeply and pervasively within us that kicking it out takes a lifetime of progressive sanctification. In point of fact, the sin-nature has *always* been a parasite. Even in the case of unregenerate unbelievers, "image bearer" is more basic a designation than "sinner."

Of course, this is not to say that humans are not, apart from Christ, totally depraved. They totally are. But this "new normal"—this basic sinfulness in the human race—is not essential to *humanness*. It marks something that has happened to humanity, and that something is the Fall. It is pervasive, deep, and roots into every single aspect of every human being, but we cannot say that it is essential to the ontology of humans. If we do, we would have to say in the same breath that Adam and Eve before the Fall—or Jesus Christ, along with all the elect after they are glorified—are somehow subhuman. The difference between an unregenerate sinner and a regenerate saint (i.e., *Christian*) is that the sinner's identity as image bearer has been (apart from a miracle) irreversibly marred—to the point of scarce recognition—by sin and the sin-nature, whereas the saint's identity as image bearer has been, is being, and will be restored and enhanced in Christ (2 Cor. 3:18). The Christian's most basic identity is that he is *in Christ* (Eph. 1:3–14; Rom. 6:5–6; Gal. 2:20; Col. 3:1–4). That, most *fundamentally*, is who the Christian is.

Now, what in the world does all of this have to do with sinful impulses and the cultivation of the shameless confession thereof? Simply this: *we don't lose anything worth holding onto when we confess sinful, disgusting, disturbing impulses.* What do we lose? Pride, the impression that we are above sinful inclinations, and maybe the esteem of others that we were inadvertently (or maybe even intentionally?) stealing from God. *Good riddance.* None of those things are essential to who we truly are in Christ. They are layers of dragon skin—we should be happy to let Aslan tear them away. But who we really are remains untouched when we confess our sinful inclinations. Our new reality means that the very best parts of us are in and from Christ, and this will only increase throughout eternity. Our truest self is our self in Christ, so letting people see the worst parts of ourselves is no problem because those parts are parasitical and not essential to our nature. When we confess our sinful impulses, we're letting people see a transient reality that is on its way out the door. In this way, when I confess my sinful impulses I'm just as much of a spectator as my brothers and sisters are. "Ugh! Did you see that? Thank God this sinful fless is temporary."

This is why we need church cultures where Christians can feel safe not only to confess sin, but also sinful inclinations. "I am attracted to the same sex." "I desire what does not belong to me." "I sometimes want to harm myself." In cultures of confession, we can be reminded by one another that these desires, if we are in Christ, are not reflective of who we truly are. This is important for us to hear because our sinful inclinations can often feel so primal and basic to who we are that we come to believe the lie *that we are our sinful desires.* And by the way, we don't need any help convincing ourselves of this false idea; that's exactly the script we're fed from our culture. We're told "You are what you want. That is the sum total of your person. Embrace it. If you try to fight it, you're not being yourself—you're doing self-harm. If others tell you that you are sinning, they are rejecting the very root of your personhood—love and disapproval are irreconcilable terms."

But in the church where confession of sinful inclinations is welcome, we receive a course correction. *That* narrative is debunked and replaced with a deeper, truer one. We get to hear our brothers and sisters say, "Those desires aren't the true you—the 'you' that you are in Christ, the 'you' that you are being continually conformed to, and the 'you' that you are promised to be, unhindered by sin, in glory." In the church where confession of sinful inclinations is welcome, we are reminded of how puny our culture's vision of humanity is. *Really? That's all we are; our sinful desires? Humans are just hunks of flesh wanting that which God calls sin? How pathetic.* The gospel message that confronts us and calls our sinful inclinations *sinful* dignifies us—it calls us so much more than our impulses.

The irony about the culture where confession of sinful impulses is not welcomed—where sinful inclinations are talked about in hushed voices—is that those cultures are the most hospitable places for sin! Sin and the sin-nature are like cockroaches: they love the dark. So when you foster the kind of culture where the expectation is for the confession of sinful impulses to be met with gasps, shame, and condemnation, you are leaving the lights off. The cultures that *seem* the most offended by sin are often the cultures that are most hospitable to sin. But the culture that invites the confession of sin and sinful impulses turns the lights on, sweeps the floor, and lays out poison traps. A culture of confession is inhospitable to sin.

Another benefit of cultivating a culture where confession of sinful impulses is welcomed and invited is that practical, real-time growth becomes more of a realistic possibility. Why is this? Because when we take aim at the desire to sin, we are taking aim not at the fruit, but the root. Confessing sin and confessing the desire to sin is the difference between cutting down a weed and ripping it out. When we start to get out of the habit of only confessing (to God and to others) after *acting* upon sinful desires, and start to get into the habit of confessing (to God and to others) the desires themselves, we will begin to see something happen with our hearts. It's not magic, it's not "therapy," and it's not "choosing to live your best life now," rather, it's offering up deeper chambers of your heart to Christ, to be placed under his lordship. If we get into the habit of confessing our sinful impulses, we will find ourselves almost perpetually in a state of prayer for strength and holiness. We will find our awareness of our neediness for the Holy Spirit's ministry heighten to a degree we never previously thought possible. And this, my friends, is nothing short of grace.

Confession of sinful impulses is one of God's gracious means for cultivating intimate communion with him.

If the grace of God had nothing to say about our sinful inclinations, and nothing to offer us by way of resources, it would be of no present good to any of us. But, thanks be to God that his grace isn't limp. His grace has a backbone. His grace doesn't offer us forgiveness for our sins and hope for heaven *alone*. Praise God that his grace "has appeared, bringing salvation for all people, *training us to renounce ungodliness and worldly passions, and to live self-controlled, upright, and godly lives in the present age*, waiting for our blessed hope, the appearing of the glory of our great God and Savior Jesus Christ, who gave himself for us to redeem us from all lawlessness and to purify for himself a people for his own possession who are zealous for good works" (Tit. 2:11–14, emphasis mine).

About the Author

Samuel G. Parkison (PhD, Midwestern Seminary) is Associate Professor of Theological Studies and Director of the Abu Dhabi Extension Site at Gulf Theological Seminary in the United Arab Emirates, where he lives with his wife (Shannon) and their three sons (Jonah, Henry, and Lewis).

Before coming to GTS, Samuel was Assistant Professor of Christian Studies at Midwestern Baptist Theological Seminary, and Pastor of Teaching and Liturgy at Emmaus Church in Kansas City, Missouri. Samuel writes and researches on a broad range of topics, including Trinitarianism, Christology, soteriology, aesthetics, and philosophy of a religion, as well as many issues pertaining to cultural engagement and ethics.

He is the author of *Revelation and Response: The Why and How of Leading Congregational Worship Through Song,* as well as the forthcoming volume, *Irresistible Beauty: Beholding Triune Glory in the Face of Jesus Christ.*

Samuel blogs regularly at his website, *words matter* (samuelparkison.wordpress.com).
Follow him on Twitter @samuel_parkison.

Scripture Index

Old Testament

Genesis

New Testament

CPSIA information can be obtained
at www.ICGtesting.com
Printed in the USA
BVHW062351300522
638444BV00015B/739